Umpires : Classic Baseball Stories
from the Men Who Made the Calls

Umpires

Classic Baseball Stories from the Men Who Made the Calls

JOHN C. SKIPPER

McFarland & Company, Inc., Publishers
Jefferson, North Carolina, and London

Frontcover: Umpire Ken Burkhart signals Cincinnati's unseen Ty Cline out in the first game of the 1970 World Series. Catcher is Baltimore's Elrod Hendricks. United Press International Photo.

British Library Cataloguing-in-Publication data are available

Library of Congress Cataloguing-in-Publication Data

Skipper, John C., 1945–
    Umpires : classic baseball stories from the men who made the calls
/ John C. Skipper.
        p.   cm.
    Includes bibliographical references and index.
    ISBN 0-7864-0364-0 (sewn softcover : 55# alkaline paper) ∞
    1. Baseball—Umpiring—United States—History.   2. Baseball
umpires—United States—Anecdotes.   I. Title.
GV876.S55   1997
796.357'3'0973—DC21   97-7447
                                                                   CIP

Manufactured in the United States of America

McFarland & Company, Inc., Publishers
    Box 611, Jefferson, North Carolina 28640

For James K. Skipper III
and John F. Skipper

Table of Contents

Table of Box Scores

Introduction

For me, the story of umpires begins a long way from the old familiar bastions of baseball like Wrigley Field in Chicago or Fenway Park in Boston—and far from the 1990s parks that ooze neon, noise and shopping mall mentalities.

The first umpire I ever became acquainted with was not even a person. It was a basement window that was directly behind "home plate" in the backyard of my boyhood home in Oak Park, Illinois.

My brothers and I would play "whiffleball" in the yard; our house made a terrific backstop behind home plate. A basement window was situated so that its dimensions were just about from the knees to the shoulders of the young batters who stood in front of it.

Thus, the strike zone was the window: If a batter took a pitch and it hit the window, it was a strike.

Young, imaginative pitchers would sometimes lob a pitch six or eight feet in the air and have it float down in such a way that it would catch a corner of the window. It was an impossible pitch for a batter to hit as it dropped lazily against the window after floating past the batter about head high. It was a strike, though, and there was no arguing with this umpire.

Years later, as a young adult, my image of the umpire shifted to the little ballparks that dot most every community across the country, in leagues that exist only because mamas and papas volunteer to work the scoreboard (if there is one), work in the concession stand (if there is one), rotating shifts, of course, so they can always be free to watch their own kids' games, and yes, even take turns at umpiring—because the price for their services is exactly what the league can afford.

I remember in particular that it was in just this sort of setting that Brantley Bond, a waterbed salesman by day, stood along the foul line just behind third base, with his arms folded across his chest, as the late afternoon sun beat down on the playing field of a softball diamond in Alexandria, Louisiana, one day years ago.

The image is as clear to me as a Norman Rockwell painting: A tall, swarthy man, with a thick growth of beard that spread like a shadow across his lower face, a man built like a lumberjack and sturdy and as immovable as an oak tree as he stood by that foul line. Like a man with a mission.

Two softball teams were competing on that field, both made up of elementary school girls; all decked out in colorful cotton shirts with the names

1

of team sponsors emblazoned across them—names like Rapides Bank and Allen Glass Co.; all with baseball caps so snug on their collective heads that they were sweat-stained; and all performing to the best of their abilities while parents and friends, sitting in lawn chairs that formed a semi-circular ring behind home plate and stretching to first and third base, cheered them on.

Alexandria, like many southern towns, bloomed in late afternoon in the summertime, when the sun wasn't quite so hot. It was a town where children were taught to say "Yes, sir" and "Yes, ma'am"—and to catch a ball with two hands. By 5 P.M. in many households, it was time to start getting ready to go to the ballpark.

The city once had a minor league team—the Aces, a farm team of the San Diego Padres—and one of its pitchers, Randy Jones, later won a Cy Young Award in the National League. But the Aces were long gone now and Alexandria ... well, it was a softball town, with a season that started in what would be late winter in many parts of the country. Hardly anybody fretted about the number of games and practices held on "school nights." Instead, men in office buildings would compare notes on the season records of their kids' teams while women, upon seeing each other in grocery stores, would ask things like: "Who are y'all playin' tonight?"

It was in exactly this type of environment that Brantley Bond, waterbed salesman by day, stood like a centurion along the third base line.

Late in the game, a little ponytailed slugger took a mighty swing with her gray, metal bat and soundly smacked the whirling white ball coming at her from the pitcher's mound. The ball zipped off the bat with the speed of a marble in a pinball machine.

It never got more than a foot off the ground and it must have seemed like a bullet to the third baseman, who acted more intently on getting out of the way than in catching the ball.

Then, suddenly, just as fast as it had left the bat, it dropped, halfway into left field but an inch or so foul—or was it fair? It was so close to the foul line— was that dust from the dry soil, or was it chalk dust from the foul line that the ball had kicked up as it landed and rolled toward the fence?

The batter had dropped her bat and was chugging as fast as she could toward first base, her cheeks puffed, her look determined, her eyes wide.

Meanwhile, a commotion was heard on the other side of the field, near where the ball landed. The third base coach was yelling, "Fair ball, fair ball" and the crowd of moms and dads and grandmas and grandpas and aunts and uncles behind the dugout stood and shouted, as if they had rehearsed it: "Foul, it was foul!"

And at that moment, Brantley Bond, the waterbed salesman by day, standing along the third base line in this early evening, had something in common with Bill Klem, Beans Reardon, Jocko Conlan, Babe Pinelli, Dutch Rennert and hundreds of others in the illustrious lore of baseball who are often known simply as "The Ump."

They are anonymous footnotes, frequently not even mentioned by name in the captions of some of the great photographs of the sport, and yet they all have their moment, like Brantley Bond did, as every pair of eyes in the ballpark focused on him and the cries of "Fair ball, fair ball" and "Foul, foul," echoed like the hoots of owls in the Grand Canyon.

Bond responded to the calls of the masses on that sultry softball diamond not far from the cotton fields of central Louisiana with the same sense of pride and confidence that Hank Soar and Red Flaherty had confronted an irate Billy Martin or Ted Williams on the hallowed fields of Yankee Stadium or Fenway Park. And he uttered a response often attributed to the late, great Klem that, more than anything else, defines what umpiring is all about.

"It ain't nothin' till I call it," said Brantley Bond.

That is simple, forthright testimony to the importance of the umpire, whether it be a man or woman volunteering his or her time on the playing fields of children from Spokane to Pawtucket, or working for $25 a game and carfare in the lowest levels of the minor leagues, or working behind the plate in the seventh game of the World Series.

They are—and always will be—baseball's exclamation points because … they make the calls.

They are not anonymous. Indeed, you will find an appendix starting on page 152 of this volume that lists them all. And yet, think about it. If Babe Ruth or Willie Mays or Reggie Jackson or Randy Johnson walked down a street toward you, you would probably recognize any one of them instantly.

But what if Red Flaherty or Dutch Rennert or Doug Harvey or Don Denkinger walked down that same street? They would go unnoticed.

They lose anonymity only when something goes wrong, when everyone in the ballpark—and in the television audience—knows he "blew the call."

Denkinger, a longtime American League umpire, knows the feeling. In the following pages, Denkinger explains how his controversial call in the 1985 World Series occurred … and the aftermath of it, including threats against his family.

Also, Bill Kinnamon reflects on the toughest call an umpire has to make and gives an example of how an ump can make a bad situation worse after missing a call.

And John Rice, a World Series umpire three different times, remembers how one of his calls resulted in the construction of an addition to an outfield wall in Pittsburgh.

Television replays often show long home runs, great plays at the plate and diving catches in the outfield. But when was the last time ESPN ever had a slow-motion replay of a great call by an umpire? The answer: hardly ever. The reason: "Cause there's so many of 'em," says Denkinger.

One of the surprising revelations for the author in completing the research for this book was learning about the number of injuries umpires receive that stay with them. Two of those interviewed sustained injuries on the field that ended their careers. And the injuries don't always heal.

"I can hardly walk," said former American League umpire Terry Cooney, three years after his retirement.

Umpires' candor and the vivid "instant replays" from their memories are what this book is all about. An author's name is affixed to this work but there are many co-authors in spirit and in deed to make a collection of memories such as this possible.

Each story in *Umpires* is a "living history"—umpires recalling what it was like to be there when some of baseball's finest moments occurred.

The research was not without its disappointments. Paul Runge, John McSherry and Augie Guglielmo were all subjects for interviews I had planned for the book.

Runge, who is still a National League umpire, turned me down politely. He wished me well with my project but said he would prefer to go on doing his job with as little fanfare as possible. His father, Ed, an American League umpire for 17 years, is featured in the book.

McSherry collapsed on the field in Cincinnati and died of a heart attack on April 1, 1996. I learned of his death while I was at work in the newsroom of the *Mason City Globe-Gazette*. In my briefcase was a note I had written with McSherry's name and how I could contact him at his home in Dobbs Ferry, New York.

Guglielmo, who spent one year in the Majors and was a partner of Steamboat Johnson in the minors, died in February 1996 at the age of 83 before I could interview him.

Every effort was made to field the best team in *Umpires*—a team consisting of accurate facts, figures, depictions of events, and attitudes and personalities of the umpires involved. The author hopes that readers will not find instances where they believe I "blew the call" in either omission of pertinent information or interpretation of it. To any who might question any of my calls, I can only say with sincerity, like Bill Klem, "I never missed one in my heart."

I thank God for providing me with the necessary gifts to complete this book.

Thanks to the staff of the National Baseball Library at the Hall of Fame in Cooperstown and especially to Bruce Markusen for always quickly and efficiently coming up with the data I requested of them.

Special thanks to Andy Alexander of the Mason City Public Library for being a good sounding board, resource and source of encouragement.

Thanks to Michael Grandon for being such a good friend and a good listener. He heard most of this book long before he had a chance to read it.

I am indebted to a family that encouraged me and provided the patience, love and support without which not only would a book like this be impossible, but little else would have meaning in my life.

And, of course, I extend my gratitude to the wonderful men who are the subjects of this book, many of them journeying into the sunsets of their lives, for graciously sharing their memories and thus becoming a part of the "living history" recorded on the following pages.

They are, after all, the men who made the calls.

John C. Skipper
Mason City, Iowa
April 1997

John "Red" Flaherty
American League: 1953–1973

Roger Maris's 61st Home Run

"Pete Runnels looked at me and said,
'I don't care what anybody says.
It tingles the spine.' I had to agree."

FALMOUTH, Mass.—John "Red" Flaherty doesn't get around like he used to.

Slowed by a stroke he suffered a few years ago, Flaherty, 77, sees baseball games now only from in front of a television set.

He is a pleasant man, quieted by the illnesses of age, and he speaks with a gentle Boston brogue that makes the listener think he's talking with the guy on the next bar stool at "Cheers."

For 21 years, Flaherty was an American League umpire, and when asked today if he misses it, his answer is instantaneous: "Sure."

He had the remarkable good fortune of being in the right place at the right time many times in his career, as he was on October 1, 1961, in Yankee Stadium.

It was the last game of the season and New York Yankee right fielder Roger Maris had 60 home runs, tying him with Babe Ruth for the most hits in a single season.

He had four, perhaps five more at-bats to try to hit number 61.

The opponent was the Boston Red Sox. The opposing pitcher was rookie Tracy Stallard. And the first base umpire was John Flaherty in a game he'll never forget.

"Maris was a helluva ballplayer," said Flaherty, "and he never got the credit he deserved."

In his first at-bat against Stallard, Maris was fooled on an outside pitch and hit a lazy fly ball to left field for an easy out.

His next time up, in the fourth inning, the first pitch to him was high and outside, the next one low and inside. The Yankee Stadium crowd of 23,154 booed as if to say in unison: "Give him something to hit."

John Flaherty had good view of Roger Maris's 61st home run.

Stallard's next pitch was a waist high fastball that Maris turned on and cranked deep to right.

Flaherty turned and started to move toward right field to signal "fair" or "foul" but there was no need. The ball was hit to straightaway right and landed about ten rows up in the right field seats.

In one swing, Maris had done what no other man in baseball history, not even Babe Ruth, had ever accomplished in one season: hit 61 home runs.

"Pete Runnels was playing first base for the Red Sox," said Flaherty. "He looked at me and said: 'I don't care what anybody says—it tingles the spine.' I had to agree," said Flaherty.

Two years earlier, on June 27, 1958, Flaherty was the first base umpire in a game between the Chicago White Sox and Washington Senators at Comiskey Park in Chicago.

Billy Pierce, the left-hander who started for Chicago, was just 6-5 for the season but was on a roll. He had pitched two consecutive shutouts.

On a hot, sticky night, he mowed down the Senators, one after another, in a duel with Washington starter Russ Kemmerer. After eight innings, the White Sox had a 3-0 lead—and Pierce was working on a perfect game, having retired the first 24 batters.

Ken Aspromonte and Steve Korcheck were easy outs to start the ninth. Washington manager Cookie Lavagetto—who 11 years earlier had broken up Floyd Bevens' no-hitter in the ninth inning of a World Series game—called on Eddie Fitzgerald, a reserve catcher, to pinch hit for Kemmerer.

Pierce started him with a curveball around the outside corner. Fitzgerald "kind of flicked his bat at it," said Flaherty. The ball, hit like a sliced golf ball, looped above the head of the first baseman. "He reached out and almost caught it," said Flaherty.

Once past the first baseman, it was just a question of whether the ball would drop fair or foul.

Fair. By inches. Flaherty made the call.

"It almost hit the foul line. It was close. Too bad for Pierce. Pierce was a nice guy. It always happens to the nice guys," he said.

Three years before that, Flaherty was across the field—on the left-field side—in the seventh game of the 1955 World Series. The Brooklyn Dodgers, seeking their first world championship ever, led the Yankees 2-0 behind the pitching of lefty Johnny Podres, when the Yankees mounted a threat in the sixth inning.

Billy Martin walked. Gil McDougald then beat out a bunt. The next batter, Yogi Berra, hit a line drive into the left field corner. Dodger left fielder Sandy Amoros, playing Berra straightaway, had a long way to run. He raced over and at full speed made a leaping stab at the ball ... and caught it. Flaherty was right there to make the call.

"A great catch it was," he said. "And then I think McDougald was doubled up." Flaherty's memory hadn't failed him in recalling that game of 40 years ago. Amoros fired the ball to cutoff man Pee Wee Reese, who whirled and threw to first baseman Gil Hodges to double up McDougald.

That ended the last serious Yankee threat and three innings later, the Dodgers celebrated their first World Series championship.

Flaherty's umpiring career took him through five minor leagues plus some winter ball in Puerto Rico—with time out for service in World War II—before finally making it to the Major Leagues.

"Why did I become an umpire? Because I was a frustrated ballplayer," he said. "I was a first baseman in high school and college but never played any pro ball.

"In the late 1930s I got a chance to go to Bill McGowan's umpire school. The first couple of weeks we were in Jackson, Mississippi, and then we went over to Florida for about two weeks," said Flaherty.

"I got my first contract in 1939 in the Pony League, Class D ball. Then I spent a couple of years in the Class C Mid-Atlantic League, then two years in the New England League. The next year I worked Class A ball in the Eastern League and after that I went to the International League, which was Triple A," he said.

In 1940, in the Mid-Atlantic League, Flaherty met a young, mild-mannered man who was in his first year as manager of the Portsmouth club. Their paths would cross 15 years later in the World Series. The manager was Walter Alston, who would later manage the Brooklyn and Los Angeles Dodgers for 24 years.

Umpiring in the minor leagues was not an easy life, Flaherty recalled. "It could get kind of rough in the minor leagues sometimes. Fans throwing things out on the field, waiting for you after the game, that sort of thing. I never got hurt but I remember in the Mid-Atlantic League in 1940 and '41, we used to go to Youngstown, Ohio, and I worked with an umpire by the name of Coleman James. His son was the athletic director at the college there and he used to bring over a bunch of football players to protect us at the games. That was what life was like in the minor leagues—for about $300 a month."

He got the call to come to the big leagues in 1953 and he credits American League umpire Bill Summers as someone who helped his career. "He contacted McGowan about me for the umpiring school and was a big help to me all along the way," said Flaherty.

He said he didn't have a favorite ballplayer but "Ted Williams was the best hitter I ever saw and I loved to watch Luis Aparicio and Brooks Robinson field. Robinson was unbelievable sometimes."

He also had special praise for Frank Robinson. "He was the hardest working ballplayer I ever saw. He never loafed on a ballfield. An umpire can tell when a guy's loafing and he never did," said Flaherty.

And what's the toughest call for an umpire to make?

"The sweeping tag at home plate with the runner coming in. You've gotta have the right angle on it. If you don't get a good shot at it, it's a pretty tough call," said Flaherty.

The Irishman who said he became an umpire "because I couldn't make it as a ballplayer," enjoyed his work and had some memorable conversations with ballplayers from time to time—like the one he had one day with Yogi Berra between pitches at Yankee Stadium.

"I told Yogi I wasn't infallible," said Flaherty. "Yogi said: 'What the hell does that mean?' I said that means I miss one once in a while. And Yogi said: 'Heck, you're the most infallible umpire in the whole league.'"

Oct. 1, 1961—Home run No. 61

BOSTON	ab	r	h	rbi	NEW YORK	ab	r	h	rbi
Schilling 2b	4	0	1	0	Rich'son 2b	4	0	0	0
Geiger cf	4	0	0	0	Kubek ss	4	0	2	0
Yast'mski lf	4	0	1	0	Maris cf	4	1	1	1
Malzone 3b	4	0	0	0	Berra lf	2	0	0	0
Clinton rf	4	0	0	0	Lopez lf	1	0	0	0
Runnels 1b	3	0	0	0	Bl'ch'd rf,c	3	0	0	0
Gile 1b	1	0	0	0	Howard c	2	0	0	0
Nixon c	3	0	2	0	Reed lf	1	0	1	0
Green ss	2	0	0	0	Skowron 1b	2	0	0	0
Stallard p	1	0	0	0	Hale 1b	1	0	1	0
(b) Jensen	1	0	0	0	Boyer 3b	2	0	0	0
Nichols p	0	0	0	0	Stafford p	2	0	0	0
Totals	30	0	4	0	Reniff p	0	0	0	0
					Tresh (a)	1	0	0	0
					Arroyo p	0	0	0	0
					Totals	29	1	5	1

(a) Popped up for Reniff in 7th; (b) Popped up for Stallard in 8th.

```
BOSTON      000  000  000—0
NEW YORK    000  100  00x—1
```

Errors: None. Left on base: Boston 5, New York 5. Doubles: None. Triples: Nixon. Home runs: Maris (61). Stolen base: Geiger. Sacrifice: Stallard.

	IP	H	R	ER	BB	SO
Stallard (L, 2-7)	7	5	1	1	1	5
Nichols	1	0	0	0	0	0
Stafford (W, 14-9)	6	3	0	0	1	7
Reniff	1	0	0	0	0	1
Arroyo	2	1	0	0	0	1

Wild pitch: Stallard. Passed ball: Nixon. Umpires: Kinnamon, Flaherty, Honochick, Salerno. Time: 1:57. Attendance: 23,154

October 4, 1955—Dodgers win first World Series

BROOKLYN	ab	r	h	rbi	NEW YORK	ab	r	h	rbi
Gilliam lf-2b	4	0	1	0	Rizzuto ss	3	0	1	0
Reese ss	4	1	1	0	Martin 2b	3	0	1	0
Snider cf	3	0	0	0	McDougald 3b	4	0	3	0
Campanella c	3	1	1	0	Berra c	4	0	1	0
Furillo rf	3	0	0	0	Bauer rf	4	0	0	0
Hodges 1b	2	0	1	2	Skowron 1b	4	0	1	0
Hoak 3b	3	0	1	0	Cerv cf	4	0	0	0
Zimmer 2b	2	0	0	0	Howard lf	4	0	1	0
Shuba (a)	1	0	0	0	Byrne p	2	0	0	0
Amoros lf	0	0	0	0	Grim p	0	0	0	0
Podres p	4	0	0	0	Mantle (b)	1	0	0	0
Totals	29	2	5	2	Turley p	0	0	0	0
					Totals	33	0	8	0

(a) Grounded out for Zimmer in sixth; (b) Popped out for Grim in seventh.

BROOKLYN 0 0 0 1 0 1 0 0 0—2
NEW YORK 0 0 0 0 0 0 0 0 0—0

Doubles: Skowron, Campanella, Berra. Sacrifices: Snider, Campanella. Sacrifice fly: Hodges. Double play: Amoros, Reese and Hodges. Left on base: Brooklyn 8, New York 8.

	IP	H	R	BB	SO
Byrne (1-1)	5 ⅓	3	2	3	2
Grim	1 ⅔	1	0	1	1
Turley	2	1	0	1	1
Podres (2-0)	9	8	0	2	4

Umpires: Honochick (AL), Dascoli (NL), Summers (AL), Ballanfant (NL), Flaherty (AL), Donatelli (NL). Time: 2:44. Attendance: 62,465.

Bill Kinnamon
American League: 1960–1969

The Maris Home Run: Another View

"As it turned out, I was the home plate umpire for
both Maris's 60th and 61st home runs."

LARGO, Fla.—Bill Kinnamon was scheduled to be the first base umpire
at Yankee Stadium on October 1, 1961. He had worked home plate the night
before, when the Yankees played the Orioles, so he was supposed to rotate to
first base on this, the last day of the baseball season.

In fact, he had packed up his gear for working behind the plate and put
it away, thinking he wouldn't need it again until next season. But this was a
special day—and the supervisor of American League umpires knew it.

Roger Maris, the slugging Yankee outfielder, had one more game—and
only one—to try to become the all-time single season home run champion.

Against the Orioles earlier in the week, and with Kinnamon behind the
plate, Maris hit his 60th home run, tying Babe Ruth for the most home runs
in one season.

"Cal Hubbard (umpire supervisor) came into our dressing room before
the game to talk with us," said Kinnamon, now 77 years old. "He asked me to
work behind the plate again."

Why? At the start of September, the American League had hired Al
Salerno to work the last month of the season in the umpiring crew that also
included Kinnamon, Jim Honochick and John "Red" Flaherty.

Now it was the last day of the season and the Yankees were facing the
Boston Red Sox at Yankee Stadium.

"It was Salerno's turn in the rotation to work behind the plate but Hubbard didn't think it was wise to put someone in that position when he only had
30 days experience. You figure he had only worked about four times behind
the plate," said Kinnamon.

"I don't think Alex minded. I really don't. After all, he was a rookie
umpire. So, as it turned out, I was the home plate umpire for both Maris's 60th
and 61st home runs," he said.

"There was some excitement that day, sure, but not as much as you might have thought. There were only about 17,000 people in the stands. But I think everyone was waitin' for it.

"I've seen a couple of different reports where Maris said he hit a fastball and in another he said he hit a slider. Whatever it was, it was right in his wheelhouse," said Kinnamon.

Maris flied out to left field his first time up. Then, in the fourth inning, on a 2-0 pitch, he slammed a Tracy Stallard offering—be it slider or fastball or whatever—deep into the right field stands for number 61.

"Roger had a very short swing. He could hit the ball hard but he did not hit the prodigious home runs like Mickey Mantle did," said Kinnamon.

Bill Kinnamon gave up a job with the IRS to become an umpire. He was behind the plate for Roger Maris's 60th and 61st home runs.

He said Maris was a quiet, unassuming ballplayer who might say "hello" when he first came up to the plate but would say little else. For most of the season, teammate Mantle was also chasing Ruth's record (he finished with 54 home runs in an injury-shortened season) and Kinnamon said Mantle was far more popular than Maris.

He said umpires typically do not get caught up in the excitement of ball-games as fans do, because umpires are so focused on doing their jobs and remaining impartial.

In 1951, when Bobby Thomson hit the three-run homer—"the shot heard 'round the world"—to win the pennant for the New York Giants, home plate umpire Larry Goetz brushed off the plate for the next batter, oblivious to the history that had just been made, said Kinnamon.

"Another thing about that Maris 61st home run game that people tend to forget—that was the only run of the game, probably one of the best games Stallard ever pitched," said Kinnamon.

(He was right about that. Stallard pitched in the Major Leagues for seven years, finishing with a lifetime record of 30-57. In 180 lifetime starts, he threw three shutouts. The 1-0 loss to the Yankees on the last day of the 1961 season clearly was one of his best efforts.)

Kinnamon said he made his only mistake of the day after the game was over. As he made his way to the dressing room, he ripped up the lineup card and pitched it in a trash container as was his habit after every game. That lineup card would be worth a fortune today, he said.

Kinnamon was not behind the plate but in the field six years later when he witnessed one of baseball's most devastating injuries—the beaning of Tony Conigliaro on August 18, 1967.

Conigliaro, at age 22, was already a budding superstar with an American League home run championship to his credit. He and his Boston teammates were playing the California Angels in a night game at Fenway Park when Conigliaro stepped up to the plate to face Angels right-hander Jack Hamilton.

Hamilton fired a pitch that rode in on Conigliaro and caught him flush in the face. "He didn't fall down. The force of the ball knocked him down. He went down in a heap and you knew right away it was bad," said Kinnamon. "It was awful." Conigliaro suffered several broken bones and severe eye damage. He missed all of the 1968 season, came back to have respectable seasons in 1969 and 1970 but played only parts of two more seasons, never achieving the greatness that seemed certain before the beaning.

Kinnamon said injuries—even serious ones—are hazards of the game. "I never saw anything like what happened to Ed Rapuano this year," he said. (Rapuano, a National League umpire working behind the plate, broke his collar bone when a foul tip hit him during a game in June 1996.)

"People don't realize how fast that ball comes back off the bat," said Kinnamon. "I always wore the outside protector so that would never happen." (American League umpires traditionally wore outside chest protectors that were wide and bulky, while National League umpires wore protectors inside their coat, similar to those worn in the minor leagues. Since 1987, the inside protector has been standard gear for umpires in both leagues.)

Kinnamon said another memorable game in his 10 years as a Major League umpire occurred in the 1968 World Series between the Detroit Tigers and St. Louis Cardinals—the only World Series he ever worked.

"The rotation had me behind the plate in the fourth game with the two best pitchers in all of baseball facing each other: Denny McLain and Bob Gibson," said Kinnamon.

During the regular season, the Tigers' McLain became the first pitcher in 34 years to win at least 30 games in one season, finishing with a 31-6 record and a 1.96 earned run average.

Gibson was 22-9 with a 1.12 earned run average, the lowest ERA for a starting pitcher in baseball history. Thirteen of his wins were shutouts.

Not surprisingly, McLain and Gibson won both the Most Valuable Player and Cy Young awards in their respective leagues.

In the first game of the World Series, the two matched up in a game dominated by Gibson, who struck out a series-record 17 in a 4-0 Cardinal victory. Detroit tied the series at a game apiece with an 8-1 victory in the second game behind lefthander Mickey Lolich. The third game went to St. Louis, 7-3, setting the stage for another McLain-Gibson classic matchup in game four, with Kinnamon behind the plate.

"Everyone thought it would be a great one but it deteriorated into a nothing game," said Kinnamon. "It ended up 10-1 or 10-2, something like that." (*Editor's note:* The Cardinals won, 10-1.)

The start of the highly-touted game was delayed by rain for 35 minutes. When play finally started, thoughts of a double shutout were erased quickly.

"I remember the young guy for the Cardinals who could run so well, Lou Brock, led off the game with a long home run off McLain," he said.

The Cardinals added another run in the first, aided by a Tiger error, and then scored twice more in the third inning before more heavy rains caused a 74-minute delay. When play resumed, McLain was gone—relieved by Joe Sparma, who served up a home run to Gibson. A four-run Cardinal eighth inning iced it.

"It just didn't turn out to be what everyone hoped it would be," said Kinnamon.

Kinnamon grew up in football country—Lincoln, Nebraska—and was a quarterback for the University of Nebraska. His college career was interrupted when his National Guard unit was mobilized at the start of World War II.

Four years later, his athletic eligibility had run out but his interest in sports hadn't. By now, he was employed as an IRS agent but, on a lark, he decided to respond to an ad he saw in *The Sporting News*, seeking students for Bill McGowan's umpiring school in Florida.

Kinnamon spent seven years umpiring in the minor leagues, beginning in the Sooner State League (Class D) in 1953, when he was 34 years old. He progressed the next year to the Pioneer League (Class C) and then to the Eastern League (Class A) where he remained for a year-and-a-half.

In June 1956, he hooked on as an umpire in the American Association and remained there until he got the call to the big leagues in September 1960 to work the last 23 games of the season. In 1961, when the American League added two more teams, more umpires were needed and Kinnamon stayed on.

He said his first game as an American League umpire came in Kansas City in 1960. "I was at third base," he said, "and I didn't have a play all night. Not one. In about the sixth inning, someone hit one down the left field line about 30 feet foul. I ran over and waved my arm, signaling 'foul ball' as if it was a big deal, just to have something to do."

Kinnamon said during one off-season he was part of a contingent of ballplayers and umpires who spent three months in Europe conducting schools on various facets of playing and umpiring.

"Whitey Ford was one of the ballplayers. We spent a lot of time together, going to banquets and that sort of thing, and we got to know each other a little," said Kinnamon.

Even 30 years later, he seemed to want to stress that they did not become friends—the implication being how unethical that would be for a player and an umpire—but they did develop an acquaintanceship.

"About a year or two later, we're in Comiskey Park in Chicago," said Kinnamon. "I'm behind the plate. By this time Whitey was getting near the end of his career. As he's coming off the mound between innings, he looks at me and says, 'Hey Bill, don't throw the dark ones out too soon, now.' Whitey had a habit of darkening the ball on one side better than anyone I ever saw. To this day, I don't know how he did it.

"I do know that sometimes the ball came up to the plate looking half black and half white," said Kinnamon. "One day Ford was pitching and I was umpiring at second base. I asked Bobby Richardson how Ford got the ball so dark. Bobby said, 'I've been playing behind him for ten years and I still don't know'."

Ford's longtime battery mate was Yogi Berra, "the best catcher I ever saw handling a ball in the dirt," said Kinnamon. "Nobody did it better than Yogi. I never, ever saw a ball in the dirt get by him."

Kinnamon said Yogi's reputation as a talker was well-earned. "One day, the Yankees were playing Boston and Sam Mele was batting. Yogi just kept talking to Mele. After every pitch, he'd start talking again.

"Finally, Mele turned around to me and said, 'Bill, can't you get this son-of-a-bitch to shut up?' And I said, 'Well, Sam, if he's talking to you, he's not talking to me'."

Kinnamon said umpires never chewed tobacco but they weren't beyond eating candy while they were on the field. "Ed Hurley always carried a lot of hard candy in his pockets. One day in Detroit, he gave me a handful before a game. I was umpiring at first base. Between innings, I gave some pieces of candy to the Tigers' first base coach.

"About the second play of the next inning, there was a close play at first and I called the Tiger runner out. There was an argument, the runner said the magic word, and I threw him out of the game. And then you know what happened? The coach reached in his pocket and threw my candy at me."

He said Billy Martin was one of the toughest competitors he ever saw. "He'd fight you tooth to toenail on the field and be a completely different guy off the field.

"He once had some kind of a job with a brewery up in the Minneapolis area. When we'd come into Minneapolis for a series with the Yankees, there would be four cases of beer in our dressing room. Four cases! They came from Billy." (Martin worked for a while as a public relations associate for the Grain Belt brewery in Minneapolis.)

"One time after one of his deliveries, Ed Hurley said to Billy, 'What are we supposed to do—carry these back to our hotel with us?' And Billy just said, 'Hey, it's a gift'."

Kinnamon retired in 1969 when an old knee injury, suffered in a serious automobile accident in his youth, caught up with him.

"I was umpiring a game in Chicago when my knee gave out and I went down. I never umpired another game," he said. Kinnamon has since had knee replacement surgery.

After his retirement, he worked for four years in an umpire development program and then ran umpire schools for ten years before selling them to umpires Bruce Froemming and Joe Brinkman.

"I'm very proud of the fact that 54 of my students eventually made it to the Major Leagues," he said.

In an interview shortly after he retired, Kinnamon said there are several sides to umpiring:

• A personal side in not letting anyone else take control of the game.
• A physical side in being agile, able to run and able to withstand pain.
• A mental side in judging when a player or manager should be ejected from a game.

Twenty-five years later, Kinnamon reflected further on the intricacies of umpiring. He said it would be difficult to say what the toughest call is for an ump.

"Hank Soar was rated the best umpire on the bases four or five years in a row in a poll conducted by *The Sporting News*. They've stopped doing it now because it caused some hard feelings—but Hank was good on the bases. He just seemed to have a knack for it.

"I know one thing. You're working your tail off when you're working behind the plate. You have to make a lot of calls and they're all important."

And, Kinnamon said, a home plate umpire has to have a high pain threshold because he's likely to get hit with four or five foul tips a game going 100 miles an hour.

"At first base, it's possible for a play to be a tie," he said. "When two things happen, they can happen simultaneously—a tie. And I'll tell you, it's a tough call for an umpire.

"But I guess the toughest call might be this: when you have to throw a guy out of a game even on a call you missed. You know you kicked hell out of the play and everyone in the ballpark knows you kicked hell out of the play but the player said the magic word and you have to throw him out. Yeah, I think that's the toughest call."

Oct. 6, 1968—Potential great pitching match-up fizzled

ST. LOUIS	ab	r	h	rbi	DETROIT	ab	r	h	rbi
Brock lf	5	2	3	4	McAuliffe 2b	4	0	0	0
Flood cf	5	1	1	0	Stanley ss	4	0	0	0

ST. LOUIS	ab	r	h	rbi
Maris rf	5	1	0	1
Cepeda lb	4	0	1	0
McCarver c	5	1	3	1
Shannon 3b	5	1	2	2
Javier 2b	4	1	2	0
Maxvill ss	4	1	0	0
Gibson p	3	2	1	2
Totals	40	10	13	10

DETROIT	ab	r	h	rbi
Kaline rf	4	0	2	0
Cash lb	4	0	1	0
Horton lf	3	0	0	0
Northrup cf	4	1	1	1
Mathews 3b	2	0	1	0
Freehan c	3	0	0	0
McLain p	1	0	0	0
Sparma p	0	0	0	0
Patterson p	0	0	0	0
Price (a)	1	0	0	0
Lasher p	0	0	0	0
Matchick (b)	1	0	0	0
Hiller p	0	0	0	0
Dobson p	0	0	0	0
Totals	31	1	5	1

(a) Struck out for Patterson in fifth; (b) Flied out for Lasher in seventh.

ST. LOUIS   2 0 2   2 0 0   0 4 0—10
DETROIT   0 0 0   1 0 0   0 0 0—1

Doubles: Kaline, Shannon, Javier, Brock. Triples: McCarver, Brock. Home runs: Brock, Gibson, Northrup. Stolen base: Brock. Double play: Cepeda and Maxvill. Left on base: St. Louis 7, Detroit 5.

		IP	H	R	BB	SO
McLain	(0-2)	2⅔	6	4	1	3
Sparma		⅓	2	2	0	0
Patterson		2	1	0	1	0
Lasher		2	1	0	0	1
Hiller		0	2	4	2	0
Dobson		2	1	0	0	0
Gibson	(2-0)	9	5	1	2	10

Umpires: **Kinnamon (AL)**, Harvey (NL), Haller (AL), Gorman (NL), Honochick (AL), Landes (NL). Time: 2:34. Attendance: 53,634.

Bill Jackowski
National League: 1953–1968

Mazeroski's Magic Moment

> "I believe it may have been the most
> exciting World Series ever."

NEW WALPOLE, N.H.—"I had the best seat in the house and I didn't
have to pay for it," laughed 80-year-old Bill Jackowski.

"Sometimes when you think you have the best seat, it turns out you can't
see a thing. But I saw it all," he said with obvious delight.

Jackowski was the home plate umpire on October 13, 1960, when Bill
Mazeroski hit a home run leading off the bottom of the ninth inning of the
seventh game of the World Series—in what many baseball observers believe
was the best World Series game of all time.

The Pittsburgh Pirates beat the New York Yankees 10-9 on Mazeroski's
homer. He thus became the first player ever to hit a game-winning homer that
ended a World Series. (The feat has only been equaled once since then, by Joe
Carter of the Toronto Blue Jays in 1993.)

"I believe it may have been the most exciting World Series ever," said
Jackowski, who was involved in some unusual incidents in his 16-year career
as a National League umpire: He once threw a Cardinal rookie out of a ballgame before the rookie had ever appeared in a game. He also had to make the
call in what is generally considered to be the strangest play in baseball history.

But in terms of memories, those two games don't even come close to the
thrill of Mazeroski's home run.

Mention Mazeroski's name to Jackowski and his first response is: "A wonderful fellow. A nicer man never played the game."

Mazeroski's heroics were the climax of a World Series that would bear
out the old cliché of a team "winning everywhere but on the scoreboard." That
was the fate of the mighty New York Yankees.

Consider: After six games, the Yankees had outscored the Pirates 46-17,
but could only manage to win three of the games, by scores of 16-3, 10-0 and
12-0. They lost three games by scores of 6-4, 3-2 and 5-2.

(Pirate reliever Elroy Face, years later, would nonchalantly shrug off the games in which the Pirates got clobbered by an average score of 13-1, saying that every time the game was close, the Pirates won!)

Well ... the seventh game was close—"It was the most exciting game of my life," said Jackowski, 35 years later.

The Pirates jumped out to a 4-0 lead after two innings but the Yankees took the lead with a run in the fifth inning and four more in the sixth. When they added a pair in the eighth to increase their lead to 7-4, the Yankees looked poised for yet another win and another comfortable victory margin.

But the Pirates scratched their way back in the bottom of the eighth, helped by a bad hop on what looked like a routine double-play ball.

"Tony Kubek was playing shortstop for the Yankees," said Jackowski. "A real nice boy from Milwaukee, Wisconsin, if I'm not mistaken." (He wasn't mistaken.)

"Anyway, the ball was coming right to Kubek when all of a sudden it jumps up and hits him right in the throat." (The ball struck Kubek on the Adam's apple and hurt him so badly that he had to leave the game.)

That play kept the inning alive and enabled reserve catcher Hal Smith to catapult the Pirates into the lead with a three-run homer. The Pirates led 9-7 at the end of eight innings.

The Yankees clawed their way back with two in the ninth—and once again, a bizarre play figured in the scoring. With runners on first and third, Yogi Berra hit a rocket of a ground ball that spun Pirate first baseman Rocky Nelson around as he fielded it. He raced to the bag to retire Berra, then looked toward second to see where baserunner Mickey Mantle was. Instead of going to second, Mantle made a dive back into first, evading Bridges' tag. While all of this was going on, Gil McDougald scored the tying run, setting up the dramatic finish.

"I remember it as if it were yesterday," said Jackowski.

Mazeroski led off the bottom of the ninth. "He took the first pitch which was high," said the old umpire.

"Then a funny thing happened. Johnny Blanchard, the Yankee catcher, called time-out and ran about halfway out toward the mound and told the pitcher, Ralph Terry, to bring it down a little.

"Well, Terry got the next pitch down and Mazeroski hit it. Yogi Berra, the left fielder, watched the ball go over his head and over the wall."

Photographs of the mob scene at home plate that day are a permanent part of the landscape of baseball history. And somewhere in that mob, making sure Mazeroski touched home plate, was Bill Jackowski.

And what was he thinking about? "I thought: Thank God, we're going home," he said.

There were many records set in that World Series, including a peculiar one in that seventh game with Jackowski behind the plate: There were no strike outs—amazing when you consider the free-swinging affair that it was, with 24 hits including a double and five home runs!

The incident in which he tossed a Cardinal out of a game before he ever played in one occurred in 1953—the rookie year for Jackowski as an umpire and for Dick Schofield as a Cardinal infielder.

Schofield had just signed with St. Louis and was in the dugout watching a game in which Cardinal manager Eddie Stanky became incensed with some calls made by Jackowski.

Stanky argued face to face, then went back in the dugout and threw some towels on the field. He motioned for others on the bench to do the same, and Schofield, the rookie, did what he was told.

Jackowski saw Schofield toss a towel and threw him out of the game. So Schofield had an ejection before he had an at-bat in the Major Leagues. An unusual circumstance, to say the least.

But nothing before or since compares to what happened at Wrigley Field in Chicago on June 30, 1959. And Jackowski was right in the middle of it.

Cub pitcher Bob Anderson delivered an inside pitch to Cardinal batter Stan Musial that sailed past Cub catcher Sammy Taylor. Home plate umpire Vic Delmore called it ball four.

Taylor thought the pitch hit Musial's bat and began a heated discussion with Delmore as the ball rolled all the way back to the wall behind home plate.

Meanwhile, Musial trotted casually to first base, made the routine turn at first—and then took off for second when he noticed Taylor still arguing with the umpire.

Alvin Dark, the veteran Cub third baseman, saw the pitch get by Taylor and hustled behind the plate to get it. When he saw Musial going to second, he fired the ball to shortstop Ernie Banks to try to make the play on Musial.

Here's where it gets interesting: At the same time Dark was making his throw to Banks, home plate umpire Delmore, still talking with Taylor, took a new ball out of his pouch and handed it to the catcher.

Jackowski, the second base umpire that day, was about to be the center of attention in baseball's most unusual play.

"The catcher said, 'Give me a ball' and Vic gave him one," said Jackowski. "I felt sorry for Vic. It could have happened to anyone."

Taylor threw the new ball to the pitcher Anderson, who saw Musial streaking for second. So he turned and threw the new ball to Banks who was in the process of catching the first ball. But Anderson threw wildly and the ball went into centerfield.

Seeing this, Musial took off for third and was promptly tagged by Banks, who was now holding the first ball. "It was a helluva mess," said Jackowski. But it was his job to make the call.

"I ruled Musial was out because Ernie tagged him with the live ball," he said. "The other ball doesn't count, just the live one.

"I got no argument except from Solly Hemus, the Cardinal manager. He was mad and who could blame him? It was a real mess.

"There was only one live ball and I saw it. I made the right call," he says today with the same conviction with which he made the call so long ago.

Jackowski frets a little because he said his memory is starting to fail him these days. "I know the plate is 17 inches wide, there are 90 feet between the bases and the pitcher's mound is 60 feet, 6 inches from home plate. Other than that, I don't know much any more," he said.

But Jackowski, who spent his off seasons refereeing college basketball games for 26 years, doesn't have any trouble remembering the top ballplayers of his day.

"Willie Mays, without a doubt, was the best all-around player I ever saw. And Warren Spahn was as good a pitcher as ever came down the line. He could have a 3-0 count and you could bet your bippy the next three would be strikes," said the ump.

Oct. 13, 1960—Greatest World Series game ever?

NEW YORK	ab	r	h	rbi	PITTSBURGH	ab	r	h	rbi
Richardson 2b	5	2	2	0	Virdon cf	4	1	2	2
Kubek ss	3	1	0	0	Groat ss	4	1	1	1
DeMaestri ss	0	0	0	0	Skinner	2	1	0	0
(d) Long	1	0	1	0	Nelson 1b	3	1	1	2
(e) McD'gld	0	1	0	0	Clemente rf	4	1	1	1
Maris rf	5	0	0	0	Burgess c	3	0	2	0
Mantle cf	5	1	3	2	Chr'pher (b)	0	0	0	0
Berra lf	4	2	1	4	Smith c	1	1	1	3
Skowron 1b	5	2	2	1	Hoak 3b	3	1	0	0
Blanchard c	4	0	1	1	Mazeroski 2b	4	2	2	1
Boyer 3b, ss	4	0	1	1	Law p	2	0	0	0
Turley p	0	0	0	0	Face p	0	0	0	0
Stafford p	0	0	0	0	(c) Cimoli	1	1	1	0
(a) Lopez	1	0	1	0	Friend p	0	0	0	0
Shantz p	3	0	1	0	Haddix p	0	0	0	0
Coates p	0	0	0	0	**Totals**	31	10	11	10
Terry p	0	0	0	0					
Totals	40	9	13	9					

(a) Singled for Stafford in third; (b) Ran for Burgess in seventh; (c) Singled for Face in eighth; (d) Singled for DeMaestri in ninth; (e) Ran for Long in ninth.

```
NEW YORK      000  014  022—9
PITTSBURGH    220  000  051—10
```

None out when winning run scored. Errors: Maris. Double plays: Stafford, Blanchard and Skowron. Richardson, Kubek and Skowron. Kubek, Richardson and Skowron.

Left on base: New York 6, Pittsburgh 1. Doubles: Boyer. Home runs: Nelson, Skowron, Berra, Smith, Mazeroski. Sacrifice: Skinner.

	IP	H	R	BB	SO
Law	5	4	3	1	0
Face	3	6	4	1	0
Friend	0	2	2	0	0
Haddix (W)	1	1	0	0	0
Turley	1	2	3	1	0
Stafford	1	2	1	1	0
Shantz	5	4	3	1	0
Coates	⅔	2	2	0	0
Terry (L)	⅓	1	1	0	0

Umpires: Jackowski (NL), Chylak (AL), Boggess (NL), Stevens (AL), Landes (NL), Honochick (AL). Time: 2:36. Attendance: 36,683.

June 30, 1959—Two balls ... and the right call

ST. LOUIS	ab	r	h	rbi	CHICAGO	ab	r	h	rbi
Blas'game 2b	5	0	0	0	T. Taylor 2b	4	1	0	0
Cunn'gham rf	5	0	1	0	Dark 3b	4	0	1	0
White, lf 1b	4	2	3	0	Noren lf	4	0	0	0
Boyer 3b	3	0	1	1	Banks ss	3	0	1	0
Cimoli cf, lf	4	0	0	0	Long 1b	3	0	0	1
Musial 1b	2	1	1	0	Thomson cf	4	0	0	0
(b) Flood cf	0	0	0	0	Walls rf	4	0	1	0
H. Smith c	4	0	1	0	S. Taylor c	3	0	0	0
Gray ss	3	1	2	1	Anderson p	2	0	0	0
Tate ss	1	0	0	0	(a) Marshall	1	0	1	0
Jackson p	4	0	1	1	Elston p	0	0	0	0
Totals	35	4	10	3	Totals	32	1	4	1

(a) Singled for Anderson in seventh; (b) Ran for Musial in eighth

```
ST. LOUIS   1 1 0   0 0 0   1 1 0—4
CHICAGO     0 0 1   0 0 0   0 0 0—1
```

Errors: Blasingame, Anderson, Elston. Assists: St. Louis 15, Chicago 12. Left on base: St. Louis 7, Chicago 4. Doubles: White. Stolen bases: Boyer 2, Gray 2, White 2.

	IP	H	R	BB	SO
Jackson (W, 7-6)	9	4	1	2	6
Anderson (L, 4-7)	7	9	3	1	6
Elston	2	1	1	2	1

Umpires: Delmore, Barlick, Jackowski, Crawford. Time: 2:35. Attendance: 9,685.

John Rice
American League: 1955–1973

The First World Series Night Game

"That dwarf selling newspapers outside the hotel
was shouting, 'I'll tell you the score of tomorrow's
game today. Chicago wins 1-0.' And he was right."

CHICAGO—If you want to get John Rice's juices flowing, just mention all the commotion over "half-swings" in today's brand of baseball. Or ask
him about the foul pole that wasn't there in the 1971 World Series, or about
the dwarf who predicted the final score of the fifth game of the 1959 World
Series.

He treasures the memories of all the World Series games he worked. And
Rice, now 77 years old, worked four of them during his 19 years as an American League umpire.

Rice's first World Series assignment came in 1959 when the Chicago
White Sox went up against the Los Angeles Dodgers. The White Sox won
the first game at Comiskey Park, 11-0, behind the pitching of Early Wynn and
two home runs by Ted Kluszewski.

The Dodgers came from behind to win the second game, 4-3—a contest
that produced one of the most famous photographs in World Series history.
Charlie Neal of the Dodgers hit two home runs in the game. On one of them,
White Sox leftfielder Al Smith backed up against the wall—and got a shower
of beer from a cup that tipped over as a fan attempted to catch the ball. A news-
paper photographer captured all of the action, including the beer in mid-
flight.

The two teams then headed for Los Angeles where the Dodgers won the
next two games. The White Sox needed to win the next one to stay alive and
to bring the series back to Chicago.

"A strange thing happened before that game. We were staying in a hotel
on the square in Los Angeles and there was a little dwarf who used to sell newspapers outside that hotel.

"The night before the fifth game, that dwarf selling newspapers outside

24

the hotel was yelling, 'I'll tell you the score of tomorrow's game today. Chicago wins, 1-0.' And he was right," said Rice.

The next day, the only run of the game was scored on a double play ball hit by Sherman Lollar. Three White Sox pitchers—Bob Shaw, Billy Pierce and Dick Donovan—combined for the shutout.

The teams returned to Chicago where the Dodgers won 9-3 to capture their first World Series title since moving to Los Angeles.

Rice thinks the best game he ever saw might have been the fourth game of the 1966 World Series between the Dodgers and Baltimore Orioles.

"It was just an outstanding game," said Rice. "It was on a Jewish holiday. Sandy Koufax would have pitched for the Dodgers but he never worked on the Jewish holiday. So they moved the big guy ... the big right-hander ... Drysdale up a day and he pitched a great game."

The Dodgers, managed by Walter Alston, were used to great pitching performances all year while Baltimore manager Hank Bauer's starters struggled to finish what they started. Koufax, in fact, had more complete games, 27, than the entire Oriole staff.

Koufax, a 27-game winner during the regular season, pitched the pennant-clinching game on the last day of the season and therefore missed the starting assignment for game one of the series. That responsibility fell to Drysdale, who gave up back-to-back home runs to Frank Robinson and Brooks Robinson in the first inning. The Orioles went on to win, 5-2.

The game is perhaps best remembered for Moe Drabowsky's 6⅔ innings of spectacular relief work after Baltimore starter Dave McNally walked the bases loaded in the third inning.

In game two, Jim Palmer set the Dodgers down 6-0 on a four-hitter and Wally Bunker tossed another shutout in game three, 1-0.

That set the stage for game four: the Dodgers once again turned to Drysdale and the Orioles countered with McNally.

"What a game," said Rice. "What a great pleasure to work that game. The Orioles won it 1-0 on a Frank Robinson home run. The whole thing was over in about an hour and 45 minutes. Boy, you don't see that anymore."

Oriole pitchers had held the Dodgers scoreless for 33 innings and threw three consecutive complete games—this from a staff that had only 23 complete games all year and whose big winner during the season was Palmer with 15.

Five years later, Rice made a call in the 1971 World Series that he says resulted in the Pittsburgh Pirates changing their ballpark.

The Baltimore Orioles were in the World Series again, and, playing in their home park, they jumped out to a 2-0 series lead with 5-3 and 11-3 victories. The scene then shifted to Pittsburgh where the Pirates won a Tuesday afternoon game, 5-1, behind the pitching of right-hander Steve Blass.

The table was set for game four, the first night game in World Series history, and a call that sticks in Rice's memory caused by something missing in the ballpark.

"The park didn't have any foul poles," said Rice. "You had the foul line on the field and then there was a fence with a yellow line on it and then about an 18-inch gap and a wall with a yellow line on it and that was it. I remember before the first game there, when we were discussing the ground rules with the managers, Nester Chylak (an American League umpire) complained about it, but what could you do?

"In the second game there, the first night game ever in the World Series, Eddie Vargo of the National League was behind the plate. I was working the right-field line," said Rice.

The Orioles jumped on top in a hurry with three runs in the first inning, sending young Luke Walker to the showers as the Pirates brought on Bruce Kison to finish the inning.

The Pirates got two of the runs back in the bottom of the first, added another in the third and one more in the seventh. Meanwhile, Kison mowed the Orioles down, allowing just one hit the rest of the way as Pittsburgh won 4-3. But the Pirates might have scored even more except ...

"In the middle of the game, Roberto Clemente hits this wicked line drive down the right-field line," said Rice. "It went into the stands right in the area where there was no foul pole. When you have to make a call like that, it's a killer-diller. I called it foul.

"Everybody told me afterward if there had been a foul pole, it would have been a home run. And the next year they put up a foul pole!" he said.

The Pirates went on to win the series four games to three. Clemente led the way with a .414 average.

Rice's umpiring career began shortly after the end of World War II. He was working at an appliance store "back in the neighborhood" in Chicago when he used the GI Bill to enter Bill McGowan's umpiring school in West Palm Beach, Florida.

"It lasted about a month and you weren't guaranteed a job when it was over. You were completely on your own. Two of the teachers were Bill McKinley and Ed Hurley, two Major League umpires.

"They would teach you positioning and how to handle various plays and we even played some ball. The last week or ten days there were people there to evaluate you and they recommended you to leagues looking for umpires," said Rice.

He worked a year in Class D ball in the Illinois State League and then moved to Class C where he spent a year in the Mid-Atlantic League and a year in the California League.

Then he moved to Class A ball and worked two years in the Western League before making the jump to the American Association—Triple A— where he spent two years before being signed by the American League.

Between two of those minor league seasons, he umpired winter ball in Caracas, Venezuela.

"It was very lonely in the minor leagues," said Rice. "You're away from home all the time and the pay wasn't good. When I started, I got $5,000 a year and $15 a day expenses—for meals and hotel rooms. Imagine trying to survive on that. A lot of guys didn't last long. It wasn't an easy life.

"Minor league fans can be tough, too. It wasn't unusual to have them throw things at you out of the stands—bottles and other things. They'd know your car, too. You'd come out after a game and find they'd let the air out of your tires."

Rice's first game in the Major Leagues was in Washington. "I don't remember who the Senators were playing but it must have been the Orioles because that would have been a cheap train ride.

"Back in those days, you always had the season opener in Washington and the president would be there ... and it would have been a cheap train ride back to Baltimore.

"I don't remember anything in particular about that game except that the three other umpires were all senior umpires—Ed Rommel, Charlie Berry and Bill Summers—and so I was at second base. It used to be that when you broke in, they always put you at second base."

Reflecting back on his career, Rice said, "It's not a real easy life. You don't make friends with the ballplayers and you don't have favorite ballplayers. When you're in the minor leagues, you learn some lessons. And one of them is: You don't have favorite ballplayers. If you do, you might not make it up to the big leagues.

"It seems like the only people you get along with are your fellow umpires and sometimes that doesn't work out. It's hard living and traveling with three other guys for that long a time. And if it does work out, sometimes they break you up just to make the others happy, the ones that aren't getting along so well."

(Rice's point about getting along with fellow umpires was illustrated, in another context, by longtime National League umpire John "Beans" Reardon. Upon receiving the Bill Klem Award for umpiring in 1970, long after he retired, Reardon told his audience: "I'm very glad to receive the Klem Award but I'll tell you the truth: Klem hated my guts and I hated his.")

Rice said he didn't have a favorite ballpark. "The backgrounds in ballparks are all different—and what can you do about it? Nothing. So you just go with it.

"A lot of the umpires used to complain about the ballpark in Kansas City. Right behind the left center field wall there was a highway and it seemed like just as the pitcher was going into his windup ... here comes a truck moving across your line of view. You had to really concentrate," he said.

Rice said he thinks the toughest call for an umpire is the tail end of a double play at first base. "It's always close and you've got to be right on it.

"The most important thing is to get in position to see the ball in flight and follow it to the glove. You hear some people say you go by sound, the sound of the ball hitting the glove. Baloney. You go by sight," he said.

"Everyone used to cry about the half-swing. That was a tough call. Now it's a joke. Everyone can appeal it. The catcher can appeal. The pitcher can appeal. It's a joke."

Rice pointed out that appeals are made only when the umpire rules the half-swing was no swing. "If you call it a strike, there's no appeal, and you can't take it back. It's a strike," he said.

He said today's fans may have the impression that ballplayers were playing for the love of the game back in the days when Rice umpired.

"Actually," he said, "I think they were a little meaner then. They just acted like they were playing for fun."

October 6, 1959—The dwarf was right!

CHICAGO	ab	r	h	rbi	LOS ANGELES	ab	r	h	rbi
Aparicio ss	4	0	2	0	Gilliam 3b	5	0	4	0
Fox 2b	3	1	1	0	Neal 2b	5	0	1	0
Landis cf	4	0	1	0	Moon cf-rf	4	0	1	0
Lollar c	4	0	0	0	Larker lf	4	0	0	0
Klu'ski 1b	4	0	0	0	Hodges 1b	4	0	3	0
Smith rf-lf	4	0	0	0	Demeter cf	3	0	0	0
Phillips 3b	3	0	1	0	(e) Fairly	0	0	0	0
McAnany lf	1	0	0	0	(f) Repulski rf	0	0	0	0
Rivera rf	0	0	0	0	Roseboro c	3	0	0	0
Shaw p	1	0	0	0	(g) Furillo	1	0	0	0
Pierce p	1	0	0	0	Pignatano c	0	0	0	0
Totals	28	1	5	0	Wills ss	2	0	0	0
					(a) Essegian	0	0	0	0
					(b) Zimmer ss	1	0	0	0
					Koufax p	2	0	0	0
					(c) Snider	1	0	0	0
					(d) Podres	0	0	0	0
					Williams p	0	0	0	0
					(h) Sherry	1	0	0	0
					Totals	36	0	9	0

(a) Walked for Wills in seventh; (b) Ran for Essegian in seventh; (c) Hit into force play for Koufax in seventh; (d) Ran for Snider in seventh; (e) Announced as batter for Demeter in eighth; (f) Walked intentionally for Fairly in eighth; (g) Popped out for Roseboro in eighth; (h) Grounded out for Williams in ninth.

```
CHICAGO        000  100  000—1
LOS ANGELES    000  000  000—0
```

Runs batted in: None (Run scored on double play ball). Triple: Hodges. Stolen base: Gilliam. Sacrifices: Shaw 2. Double play: Neal and Hodges. Left on base: Chicago 5, Los Angeles 11.

	IP	H	R	BB	SO
Koufax (L)	7	5	1	1	6
Williams	2	0	0	2	0
Shaw (W)	7⅓	9	0	1	1
Pierce	0	0	0	1	0
Donovan	1⅔	0	0	0	0

Wild pitch: Shaw. Umpires: Summers (AL), Dascoli (NL), Hurley (AL), Secory (NL), Dixon (NL) and Rice (AL). Time: 2:28. Attendance: 92,706.

Sunday, October 9, 1966 — Best game ump ever saw

LOS ANGELES	ab	r	h	rbi	BALTIMORE	ab	r	h	rbi
Wills ss	3	0	0	0	Aparicio ss	3	0	1	0
W. Davis cf	4	0	0	0	Snyder cf-lf	3	0	0	0
L. Johnson rf	4	0	1	0	F. Robinson rf	3	1	1	1
T. Davis lf	3	0	0	0	B. Robinson 3b	3	0	1	0
Lefebvre 2b	2	0	1	0	Powell 1b	3	0	1	0
Parker 1b	3	0	0	0	Blefary lf	2	0	0	0
Roseboro c	3	0	0	0	Blair cf	0	0	0	0
Kennedy 3b	2	0	1	0	D. Johnson 2b	3	0	0	0
(a) Stuart	1	0	0	0	Etchebarren c	3	0	0	0
Drysdale p	2	0	0	0	McNally p	3	0	0	0
(b) Ferrara	1	0	1	0	**Totals**	26	1	4	0
(c) Oliver	0	0	0	0					
Totals	28	0	4	0					

(a) Struck out for Kennedy in ninth; (b) Singled for Drysdale in ninth; (c) Ran for Ferrara in ninth.

```
LOS ANGELES   0 0 0   0 0 0   0 0 0—0
BALTIMORE     0 0 0   1 0 0   0 0 x—1
```

Home run: F. Robinson. Double plays: Lefevbre, Wills and Parker; Aparicio, D. Johnson and Powell; B. Robinson, D. Johnson and Powell; Etchebarren and D. Johnson. Left on base: Los Angeles 3, Baltimore 2.

	IP	H	R	BB	SO
Drysdale (L)	8	4	1	1	5
McNally (W)	9	4	0	2	4

Umpires: Rice (AL), Steiner (NL), Drummond (AL), Jackowski (NL), Chylak (AL) and Pelekoudas (NL) Time: 1:45. Attendance: 54,458

Oct. 13, 1971 — Where's the foul pole?

BALTIMORE	ab	r	h	rbi	PITTSBURGH	ab	r	h	rbi
Blair cf	4	1	2	0	Cash 2b	4	1	1	0
Belanger ss	4	1	1	0	Hebner 3b	5	1	1	0

BALTIMORE	ab	r	h	rbi	PITTSBURGH	ab	r	h	rbi
Rett'mund lf	4	1	1	0	Clemente rf	4	0	3	0
F. Rob'son rf	2	0	0	0	Stargell lf	5	1	2	1
B. Rob'son 3b	3	1	0	1	Oliver cf	4	0	2	2
Powell 1b	3	0	0	1	Robertson 1b	4	1	1	0
Johnson 2b	3	0	0	0	Sanguillen c	4	0	2	0
Etchebarren c	2	0	0	0	Hernandez ss	3	0	1	0
Dobson p	2	0	0	0	(b) Dav'llo	1	0	0	0
Jackson p	0	0	0	0	Giusti p	0	0	0	0
(a) Shopay	1	0	0	0	Walker p	0	0	0	0
Watt p	0	0	0	0	Kison p	2	0	0	0
Richert p	0	0	0	0	(c) May	1	0	1	1
Totals	28	3	4	2	(d) Alley ss	0	0	0	0
					Totals	37	4	14	4

(a) Grounded into fielder's choice for Jackson in seventh; (b) Reached base on Blair's error for Hernandez in seventh; (c) Singled for Kison in seventh; (d) Ran for May in seventh.

```
BALTIMORE    3 0 0   0 0 0   0 0 0—3
PITTSBURGH   2 0 1   0 0 0   1 0 x—4
```

Doubles: Stargell, Oliver, Blair. Stolen bases: Sanguillen, Hernandez. Sacrifice flies: B. Robinson, Powell. Double plays: Hernandez, Cash and Robertson; Belanger, Johnson and Powell. Left on base: Baltimore 4, Pittsburgh, 13.

	IP	H	R	BB	SO
Dobson	5⅓	3	3	3	4
Jackson	⅔	0	0	1	0
Watt (L)	1⅓	4	1	0	1
Richert	⅔	0	0	0	1
Walker	⅔	3	3	1	0
Kison (W)	6⅓	1	0	0	3
Giusti	2	0	0	0	1

Passed ball: Sanguillen. Hit by pitch: By Kison, 3 (Johnson, F. Robinson, Etchebarren). Umpires: Vargo (NL), Odom (AL), Kibler (NL), Chylak (AL), Sudol (NL) and Rice (AL). Time: 2:48. Attendance: 51,378

Laurence "Dutch" Rennert
National League: 1973–1992

Schmidt Hits 4 Home Runs

"Umpiring at second base, I caught a cold from the
breeze caused by all those balls flying by me."

VERO BEACH, Fla.—"STEEEEEE-RIKE," shouted the umpire as he jabbed his right arm and hand out in an exaggerated signal.

It was Laurence "Dutch" Rennert's trademark for 20 years in the National League but it started a long time before that.

"I was in umpire school in the 1950s and one of the instructors there was Augie Donatelli, a great National League umpire," said Rennert, now 61 years old. "He said to me, 'Dutch, you're a little guy. You're gonna have to bounce around a little—and use your voice.'

"So I was calling out strikes like that for many years in the minor leagues. They made quite a thing of it in the majors, but I'll tell you something: Nobody ever paid any attention to it in Amarillo."

(American League umpires paid attention to it. Don Denkinger tells of an umpires association meeting in which a National League umpire was criticizing the antics of American League ump Ron Luciano. One of Luciano's American League colleagues countered by saying: "What about Rennert? When he calls a strike, he doesn't even stay in the TV screen.")

One of Rennert's favorite ballparks was Wrigley Field in Chicago, and he was involved in some memorable games there. Perhaps the most notable occurred on April 17, 1976. On that day, Rennert was the second base umpire when Mike Schmidt of the Philadelphia Phillies hit four home runs against the Chicago Cubs in Wrigley Field.

"Schmidt was as fine an all-around ballplayer as I've ever seen. He could hit, run, field and hit with power. Quite a ballplayer," said Rennert.

That Cub-Phillie game was unusual for a number of reasons. Philadelphia won it 18-16 in 10 innings and twice overcame 11-run deficits. The Phillies trailed 12-1 at the end of three innings and 13-2 at the end of four.

Schmidt homered his last four times up, including the game-winner in the 10th inning, and became the first National League player to hit four consecutive homers in the same game. All of this came after Schmidt had been dropped to sixth in the batting order (instead of his usual third) because he was fighting off a 3-for-18 slump.

The game featured 34 hits, including six doubles, two triples and nine home runs.

"Umpiring at second base, I caught a cold from the breeze caused by all those balls flying by me," said Rennert.

He reminisced about Wrigley Field: "I used to love to go there, before they put the lights in. We all did. You could live like a human being. Work during the day. Be downtown by 4 or 5 o'clock."

Rennert laments the fact he never was involved in a no-hitter. "Twenty years and I never got one. Some guys get two in a month.

"I had my share of one-hitters, though. That's gonna happen in a league with Carlton and Ryan and Seaver," he said.

One of the most unusual games he umpired—and one of the easiest—came on August 3, 1989, in a game between the Cincinnati Reds and the visiting Houston Astros. It was a day game and Rennert was behind the plate.

Cincinnati left-hander Tom Browning set the Astros down in the top of the first. Astro starter Jim Clancy was not so lucky. He faced seven batters—and all of them scored. Clancy exited without getting anybody out. Bob Forsch relieved, but the Reds' pounding continued, and seven more runs scored.

At the end of one inning, the score read: Cincinnati 14, Houston 0.

"I've never seen anything like it, but it was an easy ride, a cake walk for an umpire because it was over in the first inning," said Rennert.

When the inning was over, the Reds had amassed 16 hits in a half-inning that took 38 minutes to play. They went on to win the game, 18-2.

"I thought it would never end," said Rennert. "But games like that aren't tough. What's tough is having a knuckleball pitcher all afternoon.

"I know (Hoyt) Wilhelm was tough but the best I saw in my time was Phil Niekro. He ought to be in the Hall of Fame. When he was on his game, the batter, the catcher and the umpire were all even. You can't hit it, you can't catch it and you can't call it."

The road to the Major Leagues was a long one for Rennert. "When I was young and single, I was living in Las Vegas and that's a dangerous situation with all those gambling opportunities.

"So I started umpiring in a recreational league and there were some good teams. Military teams. And I mean they played hard ball.

"Well, there was a retired American League umpire out there named Joe Rue. One night he knocks on my door and asks if he could come in, that he'd like to talk to me. He says, 'Hey, Dutch, I've been watching you all summer. It's obvious you don't know the rules, but you've got natural ability. You ought to consider going to umpire school.'

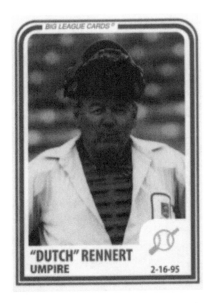
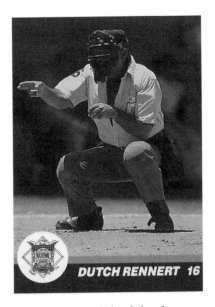

Dutch Rennert was expressive—in voice and in actions—behind the plate.

(*Editor's note:* In 1983, the *New York Times* polled Major League players to determine who they thought were the best umpires. Seventy-two percent of the players responded. In the National League, Rennert—the man who 30 years before had been told he "obviously didn't know the rules" was judged to be the best umpire.)

"I thought about it and decided to give it a try. So I went to umpire school in 1957 and became a minor league umpire the next year. I spent the next 15 years in the minor leagues.

"I think today what's true for players is probably true for umpires: If you're good, they'll find you no matter where you're working. There are scouts all over. But when I started, it wasn't that way. There was basically one supervisor for all of us and that was it.

"In the old days, you could work all year and never be seen. I worked seven years in Triple-A. To make it to that level, I must have been doing something right. And yet I was there for seven years.

"Without the help of Al Barlick, I would have never made it. Of course, he was a great National League umpire and he saw me work and he helped me. And then when I made it to the big leagues, my first crew chief, Shag Crawford, really helped me, too.

"Did you know his son, Jerry, is a major league umpire and he has another son who's a referee in the NBA? That's really something.

"My first big league game was in the old Jarry Park in Montreal. It was just a little park but it was Yankee Stadium to me. What a thrill. Everyone remembers their first game. Tom Seaver was pitching for the Mets. I was at second base. When you start out, they always put you at second base so you have two veteran umpires around you.

"I don't remember anything special about the game except that it was my first and that made it special. I do remember that during that first year, some of the players remembered me from their days in the minor leagues. I remember Tommy Helms coming up to the plate for the Reds and saying to me, 'Hi ya, Dutch, where ya been?'"

Rennert got three World Series assignments: the Philadelphia-Kansas City series in 1980; Baltimore versus the Phillies in 1983; and Oakland and San Francisco in 1989.

"You always remember your first World Series like you remember your first big league game. I remember stopping and thinking about how this is the only baseball game being played right now, and millions of people are watching," said Rennert.

"Nineteen eighty-nine was the quake series—and that was a big league quake (in San Francisco). I'd been in a couple of other quakes but never a '7.' We were in the dressing room, about eight minutes away from starting the game. It was a twilight game and they wanted it to start at 5:08 or something like that. When it hit, of course, we got out of that dressing room fast and went to the field to see what was going on. It's a good thing we had our pants on.

"I never thought they'd play that series. Here they are having candlelight meetings to figure out what to do next. I just never thought we'd play, but we did."

Rennert said Johnny Bench, Jerry Grote, and Gary Carter—all catchers and all good ballplayers—could also talk a good game, but were far different in personality.

"With Bench, if he went 0-for-4, you were the world's worst umpire and if he went 2-for-4, you were the world's greatest.

"Grote was a good catcher but he was the grumpiest ballplayer I've ever seen, a real hate-his-mother type of personality.

"And Carter ... Carter was a college type of guy. You know, 'Hi, Dutch, how's the family?' That type of thing.

"I think the funniest thing I ever saw on a ball diamond happened in a game where I'm workin' behind the plate in a game against the Mets. Dwight Gooden bunted and I made the call, I don't even remember what it was, but whatever it was, Davey Johnson, the Mets' manager, doesn't like it.

"He comes running out of the dugout and he's arguing with me and he accidentally spits his false tooth out. I see it fly out of his mouth like a bullet and it lands right by my feet.

"Well, he doesn't say anything and neither do I. And there was his tooth, right there in the dirt near home plate. He goes back to the dugout and the game goes on. A few innings later, when it's over and everybody's leaving, here comes Davey out to pick up his tooth. It's a good thing the ground crew didn't come out and drag the infield between innings," said Rennert.

He said not everybody is cut out to be an umpire. "It's not an 8-to-5 job and all the traveling can be tough. An umpire's schedule is worse than a ballplayer's. A lot of people don't realize that. Half of the schedule is home games for a ballplayer, but an umpire doesn't have a home schedule. You wind up trying to take your family with you on the road, if you can."

Rennert said the most difficult call for him was always the tag play at second base. "It was always a lot tougher for me at second than it was at first. You can't get too close or your view will be blocked. You've got to have the right angle. I had trouble with that my whole career.

"Bruce Froemming's an umpire who's always got the right angle. He can be pretty far away from the play but it doesn't matter because he always has the right angle," he said. "I think Bruce could be 30 feet away and call it right."

Rennert said one particular game in his career—September 10, 1985—symbolizes how close he came to the Hall of Fame.

"I was the home plate umpire in Cincinnati the night Pete Rose was going for his 4,193rd hit (to break Ty Cobb's all-time record). I told my wife that game would be one for the Hall of Fame.

"And you know what happened? Pete went 0-for-4. I don't think he hit one out of the infield. The next night, with Lee Weyer behind the plate, I think he hit the second pitch off Eric Show for a base hit. And the place went nuts. That's as close as I'll ever come to the Hall of Fame."

April 17, 1976—Schmidt breaks slump!

PHILADELPHIA	ab	r	h	rbi	CHICAGO	ab	r	h	rbi
Cash 2b	6	1	2	2	Monday cf	6	3	4	4
Bowa ss	6	3	3	1	Cardenal lf	5	1	1	0
Johnstone rf	5	2	4	2	Summers lf	0	0	0	0
Luzinski lf	5	0	1	0	(d) Mittw'ld	1	0	0	0
Brown lf	0	0	0	0	Wallis lf	1	0	0	0
Allen 1b	5	2	1	2	Madlock 3b	7	2	3	3
Schmidt 3b	6	4	5	8	Morales rf	3	2	1	0
Maddox cf	5	2	2	1	Thornton 1b	4	3	1	0
McGraw p	0	0	0	0	Trillo 2b	5	0	2	3
(e) McCarver	1	1	1	0	Swisher c	6	1	3	4
Underwood p	0	0	0	0	Rosello ss	4	1	2	1
Lonborg p	0	0	0	0	Kelleher ss	2	0	1	0
Boone c	6	1	3	1	R. Reuschel p	1	2	0	0
Carlton p	1	0	0	0	Garman p	0	0	0	0
Schueler p	0	0	0	0	Knowles p	0	0	0	0
Garber p	0	0	0	0	P. Reuschel p	0	0	0	0
(a) Hutton	0	0	0	0	Schultz p	0	0	0	0
Reed p	0	0	0	0	(f) Adams	1	1	1	0

PHILADELPHIA	ab	r	h	rbi		CHICAGO	ab	r	h	rbi
(b) Martin	1	0	0	0		Totals	48	16	19	16
Twitchell p	0	0	0	0						
(c) Tolan cf	3	2	2	0						
Totals	50	18	24	18						

(a) Walked for Garber in fourth; (b) Grounded out for Reed in sixth; (c) Singled for Twitchell in eighth; (d) Struck out for Summers in eighth; (e) Singled for McGraw in tenth; (f) Doubled for Schultz in tenth.

PHILADELPHIA   0 1 0   1 2 0   3 5 3   3—18
CHICAGO   0 7 5   1 0 0   0 0 2   1—16

Double plays: Trillo, Rosello and Thornton; Scmidt, Cash and Allen. Left on base: Philadelphia 8, Chicago 12. Doubles: Cardenal, Madlock 2, Thornton, Boone, Adams. Triples: Bowa, Johnstone. Home runs: Maddox (1), Swisher (1), Monday 2 (3), Schmidt 4 (5), Boone (1). Sacrifices: R. Reuschel, Johnstone. Sacrifice flies: Luzinski, Cash.

	IP	H	R	BB	SO
Carlton	1⅔	7	7	2	1
Schueler	⅔	3	3	0	0
Garber	⅔	2	2	1	1
Reed	2	1	1	1	1
Twitchell	2	0	0	1	1
McGraw (W, 1-1)	2	4	2	1	2
Underwood	⅔	2	1	0	1
Lonborg	⅓	0	0	0	0
R. Reuschel	7	14	7	1	4
Garman	⅔	4	5	1	1
Knowles (L, 1-1)	1⅓	3	4	1	0
P. Reuschel	0	3	2	1	0
Schultz	1	0	0	0	0

Save: Lonborg (1); Hit by pitch: By Scheuler (R. Reuschel), by Garber (Thornton), by Twitchell (Monday). Balk: Schultz. Umpires: Olsen, Davidson, Rennert and Vargo. Attendance: 28,287. Time: 3:42.

August 3, 1989—An extraordinary first inning

HOUSTON	ab	r	h	rbi		CINCINNATI	ab	r	h	rbi
Hatcher lf	4	0	0	0		Duncan ss	4	2	1	1
Young cf	2	0	0	0		Rich'son ss	1	0	0	0
Anthony rf	2	0	0	0		Quinones 3b	6	3	3	0
Doran 2b	3	0	1	0		E. Davis cf	4	2	3	2
Puhl 1b	1	0	0	0		Winn'ham cf	2	0	0	0
G. Davis 1b	2	1	1	1		Griffey lf	5	2	3	4
Spilman 1b	2	0	0	0		Collins lf	1	0	0	0
Caminiti 3b	2	1	1	0		Roomes rf	6	3	4	1

HOUSTON	ab	r	h	rbi		CINCINNATI	ab	r	h	rbi
Reynolds 3b	2	0	1	0		Benz'ger 1b	6	3	4	3
Ramirez ss	2	0	1	1		Reed c	5	2	4	3
Yelding ss	2	0	0	0		Oester 2b	5	1	3	2
Davidson rf	4	0	1	0		Browning p	5	0	1	0
Trevino c	4	0	1	0		**Totals**	50	18	26	16
Clancy p	0	0	0	0						
Forsch p	3	0	1	0						
Agosto p	1	0	0	0						
Totals	35	2	8	2						

```
HOUSTON      0 1 0   1 0 0   0 0 0— 2
CINCINNATI   14 0 0  0 0 0   3 1 x—18
```

Errors: Forsch. Double plays: Houston 1. Left on base: Houston 6, Cincinnati 9. Doubles: Oester 2, Duncan, Benzinger, E. Davis. Triples: Ramirez. Home runs: Griffey (7), G. Davis (24), Roomes (7), Reed (3). Stolen bases: Duncan.

	IP	H	R	BB	SO
Clancy (L, 5-9)	0	6	7	1	0
Forsch	7	18	10	0	3
Agosto	1	2	1	0	0
Browning (W, 9-10)	9	8	2	0	1

Wild pitches: Forsch, Agosto 2. Umpires: Rennert, Runge, Engel and Hallion. Attendance: 20,179. Time: 2:16

John Kibler
National League (1963; 1965–1989)

Strange Circumstances in 1984 Playoffs

"I got off the phone, jumped in the shower,
grabbed my gear, drove to the ballpark and
worked home plate in the game that decided
who was going to the World Series."

OCEANSIDE, Cal.—On October 7, 1984, John Kibler grabbed a bowl of popcorn and sat down in front of his television set to watch a college football game in his Oceanside, California, home.

It wasn't the easiest of times. Kibler, a Major League baseball umpire for 20 years, was on strike. Replacement umpires—"scabs" as he still calls them today—had been recruited to work the National League playoffs between the Chicago Cubs and San Diego Padres. That series was tied at two games apiece.

Major League umpires had been receiving $10,000 for the playoffs and $15,000 for the World Series. They wanted a pool of $340,000 to be distributed to all 60 umpires, including those who would work neither the playoffs nor the World Series—and they were sitting out the playoffs to make their point.

"It was about 11 o'clock in the morning and I was just about ready to start watching the football game when the phone rang," said Kibler, 67, who still lives in Oceanside.

"It was Paul Runge (another National League umpire.) He said 'If you come and work the plate today, Ueberroth said he'll settle the strike.' Well, what a spot that put me in."

Baseball commissioner Peter Ueberroth was in quite a spot himself. He was immensely popular because of his success as organizer of the 1984 Olympic Games held earlier that year in Los Angeles and had taken over as baseball commissioner on October 1, just as the playoffs—and the umpires' strike— were both heating up.

Ueberroth convinced both sides to accept binding arbitration, but part of the deal was that umpires would have to go back to work immediately.

"Ueberroth didn't want to use scabs in the final game. On the other hand, here it was 11 o'clock in the morning, and I was going to have to work the plate in a game that started in two hours that was going to decide the National League championship.

"I told Runge: 'That's a lot of pressure on all of us. There's a lot riding on it and if we miss any calls, everyone's going to say the scabs could have done just as good a job.' But the commissioner was trying to end the strike. Runge and Doug Harvey both lived in San Diego. I lived just 35 miles from the ballpark. And as it happened, John McSherry was in the area looking at a real estate deal. So we did it. We worked the game.

"I got off the phone, jumped in the shower, grabbed my gear, drove to the ballpark and worked home plate in the game that decided who was going to the World Series. That was the game where the Cubs seemed to have it and Leon Durham had a ball go through his legs and it was all San Diego after that."

The Cubs appeared destined to win their first pennant since 1945 when they opened the playoffs with two convincing wins, 13-0 and 4-2 at Wrigley Field. Needing only one more victory in the best of five series, they lost the first two in San Diego, 7-1 and 7-5, the second one on a dramatic two-run homer by Steve Garvey off of relief ace Lee Smith.

With Kibler behind the plate, the Cubs sent their ace, Rick Sutcliffe, 16-1 during the regular season, to the mound in the fifth and final game. Sutcliffe was the winner in Chicago's 13-0 win in the playoff opener.

The Cubs jumped out to a 3-0 lead on a two-run homer by Durham in the first inning and a solo shot by catcher Jody Davis in the second. But the Padres fought back with a pair of runs in the sixth, setting the stage for the improbable seventh.

Sutcliffe walked Carmelio Martinez to start the inning. Garry Templeton sacrificed him to second. Then Tim Flannery, pinch hitting for pitcher Craig Lefferts, bounced one through Durham's legs and the tying run scored. Allan Wiggins then dropped a base hit to left and Tony Gwynn doubled, scoring Wiggins and Flannery. Garvey, hero of the night before, then drove in the fourth run of the inning. Final score: San Diego 6, Chicago 3.

Kibler's career is dotted with incidents involving much of what will be remembered about that Cub-Padre series: union matters; showing up at games on the spur of the moment; and notable misplays, including probably the most famous situation in baseball history in which a ball went through a player's legs.

The Boston Red Sox led the New York Mets, three games to two in the 1986 World Series and appeared primed to give Boston fans their first World Series championship since 1918.

Roger Clemens, 24-4 during the regular season, started Game Six for the Red Sox, and left after seven innings with his team winning, 3-2—six outs away from a world championship.

The Mets tied the score in the eighth and the game eventually went to extra innings. Dave Henderson homered in the top of the tenth and the Red Sox added an insurance run to take a 5-3 lead.

In the bottom of the tenth, Boston righthander Calvin Schiraldi retired the first two batters; the Red Sox were one out away! But Gary Carter, Kevin Mitchell and Ray Knight all singled, closing the gap to 5-4.

The Red Sox brought in Bob Stanley to pitch to pesky Mookie Wilson, who fouled off several pitches. Stanley's seventh pitch to Wilson was wild, bringing Mitchell home with the tying run. On the tenth pitch, Wilson hit a routine ground ball that went through the legs of first baseman Bill Buckner and Knight came racing home with the winning run.

"I was umpiring at first base. I saw the whole thing. It's a shame for Buckner because he was a good ballplayer and yet that's what he's remembered for. And I thought to myself: Oh—now I've got to be behind the plate in the seventh game."

The Mets won the seventh game, 8-5, to grab the championship away from the stunned Red Sox.

"Buckner did not lose that World Series for the Red Sox," said Kibler. "There's a lot of factors that go into any ballgame. It's just like the '85 Series where people talk about the Denkinger call." (The Kansas City Royals, down three games to two against the St. Louis Cardinals, rallied in game six, aided by a controversial "safe" call at first base by umpire Don Denkinger. The Royals went on to win the game and the next night won the World Series.)

"People forget that after the Denkinger call, the next pitch is a pop up and the guy drops it. And the next pitch is a wild pitch. Denkinger didn't lose that game. People are influenced by what they see over and over again on replays but it takes more than one play or one call to win or lose a game," he said.

Kibler's quick trip to the ballpark in the 1984 playoffs was nothing new to him. His big league career started with a mad dash—again for a game involving the Chicago Cubs—but this one was halfway across the country.

"In September of 1963, I had just gotten home in West Palm Beach, Florida, from umpiring in the International League. I hadn't even gotten in the house yet. There was a telegram in the door that said: 'Be in Chicago tomorrow.'

"So I flew to Chicago and by the time I got to the park, the game had already started. I had to ask somebody where the dressing room was. I remember two of the umpires that day were Bill Jackowski and Shag Crawford. I took the field after the second inning and worked the rest of the game. I don't even remember who they were playing.

"I do remember that I had come to Chicago on the last game of a series there. So we had to drive to Milwaukee after the game. I went from West Palm Beach to Chicago to Milwaukee that fast. That's how my career started.

"When we got to Milwaukee they told me they wanted me to work the plate and that's when I discovered that in my rush to get up to Chicago, I forgot to bring my chest protector. So I had to borrow one."

He finished the season and then went back to the International League for one year—"a disappointment once you've been up in the majors, but Jocko Conlan—who they thought was going to retire—decided to umpire one more year," said Kibler. He returned to the majors in 1965 and remained through the end of the 1989 season.

"I have to give a lot of credit to Shag Crawford. He really helped me when I first started out. At one point, Fred Fleig, the National League supervisor, told me I'd have to improve if I wanted to stay and Shag really worked with me on positioning and that sort of thing. I'd have to say he saved my job," said Kibler.

Kibler grew up in upstate New York and played baseball in town leagues and in the Navy. At Norfolk, Virginia, his Navy team played against a team that had a center fielder by the name of Willie Mays.

"I had a good friend who was a ballplayer in the Yankee organization. He was a good ballplayer but he never could quite make it to the big club. He knew how much I loved the game. He told me I'd never make it as a player and said I ought to think about going to umpire school.

"Well, when I got out of the service, I went to the state police academy in New York. A lot of guys coming out of the service in those days became policemen. At the academy, I met Al Salerno, who later became an American League umpire. Salerno had a promising career as a pitcher until he fell out of a jeep in Korea and hurt himself. Anyway, I was in Salerno's room one day and I saw a book he had promoting Al Somers' Umpire School. We talked about it, decided to go ahead and go to it. We both quit the academy the same day. I had a family situation come up so we didn't go to the school at the same time. Al went in January and I went the following January. And we both wound up in the Major Leagues. Two guys from the police academy in upstate New York. That's really something," said Kibler.

"What happened to Salerno is a shame. He got fired because he tried to organize American League umpires. Al Barlick and some others had already organized National League umpires. In fact, one time they were having a meeting in Chicago and I went and they wouldn't let me in.

"Barlick and Augie Donatelli stopped me from coming in the room. They said, 'Look, we could get fired for this and you're just a rookie. Stay away from here.' They were trying to protect me. I said, 'I don't care, I'm one of you,' but they wouldn't let me in.

"Well, Al Salerno tried to do the same thing in the American League. He had a meeting and Joe Cronin found out about it and fired him. Bill Valentine tried to protect Salerno, so he wouldn't be the scapegoat. Valentine said he was at the meeting, too, and he got fired, and he wasn't even there.

"In those days, it was very, very tough. We didn't call it a union. It was an association. But it didn't matter. I know Barlick and Donatelli were trying to save me from getting fired and I know Salerno and Valentine got fired. That whole experience left a bitter taste."

Kibler said he never worked a no-hitter in his 25 years in the Major Leagues, but he came close once.

"Nolan Ryan was pitching for Houston and he had a no-hitter against the Phillies with two outs in the ninth inning and two strikes on Mike Schmidt and I'm thinking, 'Here we go, I'm going to get one.' And he throws Schmidt a great curveball and Schmidt just lays his bat out like he's fooled, like he's saying 'you got me'—and the ball hits the bat and goes for a base hit."

Kibler said he always thought the toughest call for him was the inside pitch where it was hard to determine whether the ball hit the bat or the batter.

"Oh sure, the check swing is tough, but that can be appealed. You can get help on that one. But not on the inside pitch that hits something. You're on your own," he said.

Kibler said his son is a producer for *ESPN* sports. "I have sat in the truck with them when he's producing and they can show 14 different angles of the same play. And he and his friends look at me and say: Well, what was it?

"I laugh and tell them: Hey, I'm retired."

October 7, 1984—Cubs bobble a pennant

CHICAGO	ab	r	h	rbi	SAN DIEGO	ab	r	h	rbi
Dernier cf	4	0	0	0	Wiggins 2b	3	1	2	0
Sandberg 2b	4	1	1	0	Gwynn rf	4	1	2	2
Matthews lf	2	0	0	0	Garvey 1b	3	1	1	1
Durham 1b	4	1	1	2	Nettles 3b	3	1	0	1
Moreland rf	3	0	1	0	Kennedy c	3	1	1	1
Cey 3b	4	0	0	0	Brown cf	3	0	0	0
J. Davis c	4	1	1	1	Salazar cf	1	0	1	0
Bowa ss	2	0	0	0	Martinez lf	3	0	0	0
Bosley ph	1	0	0	0	Templeton ss	3	0	1	0
Veryzer ss	0	0	0	0	Show p	0	0	0	0
Sutcliffe p	2	0	1	0	Hawkins p	0	0	0	0
Trout p	0	0	0	0	Ramirez ph	1	0	0	0
Hebner ph	0	0	0	0	Dravecky p	0	0	0	0
Brusstar p	0	0	0	0	Bevacqua ph	1	0	0	0
Lefferts p	0	0	0	0	Flannery ph	1	1	0	0
Totals	30	3	5	3	Gossage p	0	0	0	0
					Totals	29	6	8	5

```
CHICAGO      2 1 0   0 0 0   0 0 0—3
SAN DIEGO    0 0 0   0 0 2   4 0 x—6
```

Error: Durham. Double play: San Diego. Left on base: Chicago 4, San Diego 5.
Doubles: Gwynn. Triples: Salazar. Home runs: Durham, J. Davis. Stolen base:
Matthews, Sandberg. Sacrifice: Templeton. Sacrifice: Nettles, Kennedy.

	IP	H	R	BB	SO
Sutcliffe (L)	6⅓	7	6	3	2
Trout	⅔	0	0	0	1
Brusstar	1	1	0	0	0
Show	1⅓	3	3	2	0
Hawkins	1⅔	0	1	1	0
Dravecky	2	0	0	0	2
Lefferts (W)	2	0	0	0	1
Gossage (S)	2	2	0	0	2

Hit by pitch: By Gossage (Hebner); Time: 2:19; Attendance: 58,259; Umpires:
Kibler, McSherry, Harvey, Runge.

October 25, 1986 — Red Sox bobble a World Series

BOSTON	ab	r	h	rbi	NEW YORK	ab	r	h	rbi
Boggs 3b	5	2	3	0	Dykstra cf	4	0	0	0
Barrett 2b	4	1	3	2	Backman 2b	4	0	1	0
Buckner 1b	5	0	0	0	Hernandez 1b	4	0	1	0
Rice lf	5	0	0	0	Carter c	4	1	1	1
Evans rf	4	0	1	2	Strawberry rf	2	1	0	0
Gedman c	5	0	1	0	Aguilera p	0	0	0	0
Hen'son cf	5	1	2	1	Mitchell ph	1	1	1	0
Owen ss	4	1	3	0	Knight 3b	4	2	2	2
Clemens p	3	0	0	0	Wilson lf	5	0	1	0
Greenw'l	1	0	0	0	Santana ss	1	0	0	0
Shi'ldi p	1	0	0	0	Heep ph	1	0	0	0
Totals	42	5	13	5	Elster ss	1	0	0	0
					Johnson ss	1	0	0	0
					Ojeda p	2	0	0	0
					McDowell p	0	0	0	0
					Orosco p	0	0	0	0
					Mazilli rf	2	1	1	0
					Totals	36	6	8	3

BOSTON	1 1 0	0 0 0	1 0 0	2—5
NEW YORK	0 0 0	0 2 0	0 1 0	3—6

Errors: Evans, Knight, Elster, Gedman, Buckner. Double plays: Boston 1, New York
1. Left on base: Boston 14, New York 8. Doubles: Evans, Boggs. Home runs: Henderson. Stolen bases: Strawberry 2. Sacrifice: Owen, Backman, Dykstra. Sacrifice fly:
Carter.

	IP	H	R	BB	SO
Clemens	7	4	2	2	8
Schiraldi (L)	2⅔	4	4	2	1

	IP	H	R	BB	SO
Stanley	0	0	0	0	0
Ojeda	6	8	2	2	3
McDowell	1⅔	2	1	3	1
Orosco	⅓	0	0	0	0
Aguilera (W)	2	3	2	0	3

Hit by pitch: By Aguilera (Buckner). Wild pitch: Stanley. Umpires: Ford (AL), Kibler (NL), Evans (AL), Wendelstedt (NL), Brinkman (AL), Montague (RF). Time: 4:02. Attendance: 55,078.

Bill Valentine
American League: 1963-1968

The Beaning of Tony Conigliaro

"And I knew, at the very least, I had seen a man's
career end right before my eyes that night."

LITTLE ROCK, Ark.—In the summer of 1968, American League
umpire Bill Valentine was in Cleveland when he got a phone call from league
president Joe Cronin.

Valentine, now 63, can repeat Cronin almost word for word. "He said,
'Bill, this is Joe Cronin. As of today, you are no longer a Major League umpire.
The reason is that you just aren't a very good umpire.'

"I said: 'If I'm not a very good umpire, Mr. Cronin, it took you 18 years
to discover it.' And he said, 'Say hello to Ellouise [Valentine's wife] for me'
and then he hung up. That was it," said Valentine.

It marked the end of a career that began when, at the age of 18, Valentine became the youngest professional umpire in the United States. After serv-
ing an apprenticeship in the minor leagues, a chance meeting with A's owner
Charles Finley gave him the break he needed to be elevated to the Major
Leagues.

In the majors, he got to watch great stars of the era—Mickey Mantle,
Rocky Colavito, Reggie Jackson, Denny McLain and many more—and car-
ries with him today a vivid memory of being behind the plate in 1967 on the
night of a baseball tragedy in Boston.

But to fully appreciate the Bill Valentine story, it is necessary to go back
to the streets of Little Rock in the days at the end of World War II.

"I was born just seven or eight blocks from the ballpark in Little Rock—
Ray Winder Field," said Valentine. "It was named after ole Mr. Winder, who
was part of Little Rock baseball for years and years. And I'll tell you what kind
of reputation he had. Someone once said the only time he smiled was during
an eclipse.

"When I was eight or nine years old, I began working at the ballpark. The
soft drinks were all poured into cups before they were sold by the vendors so

I sorted soft drink bottles before games and I retrieved seat cushions after games and I was 'shagger'—shagging down foul balls and returning them during games."

He also looked after the umpires, and began to develop an interest in their work. He began umpiring midget league games in Little Rock to earn a little extra money.

"When I was 13, I was umpiring in the midget league. When I was 14, I was doing lower level softball games and I was doing semi-pro baseball when I was 15.

"After I graduated from high school, my grandmother paid my way for me to go to Bill McGowan's umpiring school in West Palm Beach, Florida. When I showed up down there with an inside chest protector, the guys said, 'Gees, hide that thing.' McGowan was an American League umpire who hated inside chest protectors because that's what they wore in the National League.

"The school lasted a month or five weeks and I got signed to umpire in the Ohio-Indiana League, which was Class D ball in 1951. I was 18—the youngest professional umpire ever. I didn't even shave yet. We got paid $250 a month out of which we had to pay our expenses.

"But I could eat breakfast for about 40 cents and I suppose lunch in those days was about 50 cents and you could get a good dinner for a dollar.

"In 1952 I went to the Longhorn League, which was Class C, and in '53 went to the West Texas League, which was also Class C. Joe Bauman played in that league and hit 72 home runs one year. That's still the record in professional baseball.

"I spent some time in the Big State League and the Texas League before moving to the Coast League in 1961 and 1962. Then I got signed by the American League," said Valentine.

"Charlie Finley got me into the Major Leagues. He was head of the National Tuberculosis Association and one year came to Little Rock for some promotional event. People in town hooked me up with him; I suppose because of my background in baseball.

"Before he left town, he told me to write him a complete resume of my career. I did. Later that year, I got a telegram saying my contract had been purchased by the American League.

"My first game was in Kansas City. Imagine now—I had never been in a Major League baseball park in my life and now I was umpiring in one. The rest of the crew that day was Nestor Chylak, Johnny Rice and Bill McKinley. We were sitting in the dressing room before the game when Cal Hubbard, the umpire supervisor, came in with Mr. Finley. He pointed me out to Mr. Finley and said, 'That's your boy.'

"I don't remember too much about that first game. They start you out at third base. Or at least they did in those days. You go by seniority. The senior umpire gets home plate, next in seniority gets first base, and so on.

Don Buford of Baltimore looks like he's in a hurry to get off the field as umpire Bill Valentine gives him some words of wisdom. The infielder with his back turned is the Angels' Jim Fregosi.

"The biggest thrill of my life, though, was walking on the field in Yankee Stadium for the first time. I remember coming up the ramp into the dugout and then on to the field and just looking around and thinking: 'Wow.'"

On August 18, 1967, the California Angels came into Fenway Park for a crucial three-game series with the Boston Red Sox. Valentine was behind the plate when Angels pitcher Jack Hamilton reared back and fired a pitch to Tony Conigliaro, the 22-year-old Red Sox outfielder who won the league home run championship the year before.

"Tony liked to get up over the plate. Hamilton had a reputation for throwing a spitter. I won't say he threw one then because I don't know for sure. But Conigliaro was expecting a pitch away and the ball ran in on him and I mean it really ran in on him and hit him flush in the face.

"His eye was swollen before he hit the ground. Everyone was shocked. If you could have seen his face ... Good grief. Everyone knew it was bad. Back in those days, they didn't have ambulances right at the ballpark. They just had one of those old fashioned stretchers—like a cot—in the dugout. They brought that out and carried him off.

"And I knew, at the very least, I had seen a man's career end right before my eyes that night."

Conigliaro, who had hit 104 home runs in his first three-and-a-half seasons in the majors, lost much of the vision in his left eye. He was out for the remainder of the 1967 season and all of the 1968 season.

He came back in 1969 to hit 20 home runs and hit 36 in 1970 before eye problems started to haunt him again. He retired midway through the 1971 season and in the next two decades suffered a stroke and later a fatal heart attack.

It was after the 1967 season that Valentine's troubles with league president Cronin began.

"Back in those days, baseball writers in a lot of the cities used to have big dinners in the off-season and ballplayers and umpires would go to them," said Valentine.

"Umpires came to Boston for the Boston Baseball Writers Dinner and we had a meeting the day before. We talked about how the National League umpires had already organized into an association, and they had done it with [National League president] Warren Giles' knowledge.

"Earlier in the year, we had met in Chicago and asked Bill Kinnamon to take notes. A funny thing happened at that meeting. At one point, Hank Soar stood up, looked out the window, and said, 'My God, Moe Berg's out there.' Moe Berg was a good friend of Joe Cronin's and was apparently spying on us for him."

(*Editor's note:* Morris "Moe" Berg was a major league catcher for 15 years who was as well known for his brilliant mind as for his athletic abilities. A graduate of Princeton with an expertise in foreign languages, it was said that "Berg could speak 10 languages—- and couldn't hit in any of them."

(Between the 1934 and '35 baseball seasons, Berg was part of an American barnstorming team that went to Japan for a series of exhibition games. While there, Berg drifted away from his sight-seeing teammates and secretly took photographs of Japanese buildings and other settings that were forwarded to the U.S. State Department.

(His clandestine work, unknown until years later to the ballplayers and their wives who accompanied him to Japan, was later used by U.S. military officers in planning attacks against Japan during World War II. During the war, he became one of America's most reliable intelligence agents, drawing praise for his secret activities from President Franklin D. Roosevelt himself.

(Fifteen years earlier, during the waning years of his baseball career, he was spared from retirement twice by the same man—Joe Cronin, first as manager of the Washington Senators and later with the Boston Red Sox. They became lifelong friends.

(So the prospect of Hank Soar spotting 54-year-old Moe Berg "spying" on umpires at their meeting in 1968 is rich in its historical perspective—a man experienced at spying helping out an old friend like American League president Joe Cronin.)

"Anyway, at the meeting in Boston, there were the umpires, Hubbard our supervisor, and Mr. Cronin," said Valentine. "And Kinnamon says, 'The fellows have some things they want to bring up.' And as he tries to talk, Cronin says to Kinnamon, 'You've got a lot of goddamn nerve bringing this up.' And Ed Runge says, 'Bill is not speaking for himself. He's speaking for all of us.' And Cronin got up and stormed out of the room.

"You must understand, the top salary for umpires in those days was $16,000. I had been in the league only since 1962 and I was making $12,500. So guys who had been in it twice as long as I had were only making $3,500 more. Not only was their pay unfair but they had no chance to build up much of a pension.

"Well, anyway, that's how the Boston meeting ended. At the start of the next season, I was teamed up with Jim Honochick, Frank Umont and Emmett Ashford. For some reason, Umont and Honochick just couldn't get along and so at mid-season, Honochick was switched to another crew and Al Salerno joined our crew.

"One night Salerno and I were talking about the umpires' situation. We decided to go see a guy in Oakland who was a lawyer for the National Football League. And that lawyer gave me the best advice I ever got in my life: 'Be careful or you're going to get your ass fired.'

"Well, we wound up getting a lot more legal advice. One lawyer said, 'If you're going to try to organize, do it right. Go to the National Labor Relations Board and set up a vote.' All of this time, we had been getting a lot of support from National League umpires, who were already organized.

"We set up a meeting in Chicago to talk to National League umpires. I don't remember how or why it happened, but somehow, Salerno and I got split up for a while. So he went to the meeting in Chicago and told them we were going to be mailing *NLRB* petitions to all American League umpires.

"Not too long after that, Salerno and I were back on the same crew in Cleveland when I got the call in my hotel room from Cronin, telling me to go home, that I wasn't a very good umpire. A few minutes later there was a knock on my door. It was Al Salerno. He said, 'You'll never guess what just happened to me. I just got fired.' I told him I believed it," said Valentine.

The two umpires sued the American League and, over the next few years, out-of-court settlement offers were made and rejected. "One of the offers they made was for Salerno and me to go to the minors and work some games for a week or two and then we would be recalled to the majors and be paid all the salary we missed. It would be like admitting we were bad umpires and needed to go to the minors. It was just an attempt by Joe Cronin to save face and we turned it down," said Valentine.

Eventually, they lost their court case—but at least, when the decision came, it brought closure to a matter that Valentine desperately wanted to put behind him.

(*Editor's note:* Valentine and Salerno were not the only umpires to run into some trouble for investigating the possibility of organizing. In 1945, Ernie Stewart, an American League umpire for four years, was approached by A.B. "Happy" Chandler, the new baseball commissioner, who told Stewart he wanted to look into the possibility of improving working conditions for umpires.

(According to Stewart, Chandler asked him to send a letter to every umpire in the American League with suggestions for changes in salary structure, conditions of dressing rooms and other working conditions.

(The letter got into the hands of American League president Will Harridge, who contacted Stewart and told him he wanted him to retire. Stewart resisted and insisted on a meeting with both Harridge and Chandler. At the meeting, Harridge said he had control over American League umpires and asked Stewart to sign a letter of resignation.

(According to Stewart, Chandler caved in and told the umpire he better sign it. And that was the end of Stewart's career as an umpire.

(In 1965, American League umpire Bill McKinley, among others, had a meeting with Cronin to discuss improvements in umpires' working conditions. McKinley said later the umpires hoped to organize, just as their National League counterparts had done. But they never got the chance. McKinley's contract was not renewed for the 1966 season.)

"I went back to Little Rock and started working on radio and TV. I found out I had another life," said Valentine. "I rediscovered a lot of things. Then Carl Sawatski, an old big league catcher who had been general manager of the Arkansas Travelers, got a job offer as president of the Texas League. The Travelers were Little Rock's minor league team and played in the ballpark Valentine practically grew up in.

"In 1976, I became general manager of the Travelers and have been with them ever since," said Valentine.

The attempt to organize umpires was not the only run-in Valentine said he had with Cronin.

"I was working the plate in Detroit one night and Reggie Jackson was playing right field for the A's. Fans started throwing things at him—apples, pennies, things like that.

"It was getting steadily worse as the game went on. I didn't want to make any announcements about it because I thought it would just make matters worse.

"But finally, I had to do something. In the bottom of the ninth inning, I had them announce that if it continued, the Tigers would forfeit the game. And that seemed to take care of it.

"The next day I got a call from Mr. Cronin who gave me the dickens. He wanted to know what I thought I was doing, threatening to forfeit the game. What would happen to the gate receipts, he asked. I told him I was responsible for the safety of the players and I did what I thought was best.

"There are times when umpires could have used a little backing from the league office. I am convinced that the arrogance of the 1960s brought about both the players' association and the umpires' association," said Valentine.

He is a man with a vivid memory of the tumultuous events of the past, but his recollections don't seem tinged with bitterness.

As he looked back on his abbreviated Major League career, he said one of the funniest incidents he remembers involved the Chicago White Sox. "Back then, Chicago didn't have much. So they used to put the baseballs in a freezer before the games. Or at least, that's what everyone accused them of," he said.

"We were in Chicago for a series between the White Sox and the Minnesota Twins and guys like Harmon Killebrew and Bob Allison hit some tremendous shots. And the balls just died.

"After that series, we were going from Chicago to Boston and we decided to take two of the balls from Chicago with us so someone could take a closer look at them. We put them in plastic bags and took them with us. Of course, it took a while to get there and by the time they opened them up in Boston, the stink was so bad, they had to throw them away. And what do you suppose caused the stink? Mildew. Those baseballs were mildewed. And how do you suppose they got that way?"

Valentine has had a legendary career as general manager of the Arkansas Travelers. He took over in 1976 and his team finished third for the second straight year. They finished second in 1977 and then first in 1978, 1979 and 1980.

With the help of innovative promotions, attendance at Ray Winder Field went from 116,000 in 1977 to 175,000 in 1978, 183,000 in 1979 and 216,000 in 1980. The Valentine era was prospering—and it had an ironic highlight.

In 1983, Valentine won the Larry McPhail Award for outstanding promotion of professional baseball. The award was given at baseball's winter meetings attended by most of major league baseball's top guns—including Joe Cronin.

"When I accepted the award, I thanked Mr. Cronin," said Valentine, who laughed in recalling the event. "I thanked him for the opportunity to win that award. I said that, because of him, I was in a position to get on the executive side of things at a very early age."

August 18, 1967—Conigliaro severely injured in beaning

CALIFORNIA	ab	r	h	rbi	BOSTON	ab	r	h	rbi
Cardenal cf	4	0	0	0	Andrews 2b	3	0	0	0
Fregosi ss	4	0	0	0	Adair 3b	3	0	1	0
Hall rf	4	2	2	2	Yaszst'ski lf	3	0	0	0
Mincher 1b	4	0	1	0	Scott 1b	4	0	1	0
Reichardt lf	3	0	0	0	Smith cf	4	0	0	0
Rodgers c	2	0	0	0	Conigliaro rf	1	0	1	0
Knoop 2b	3	0	1	0	Tartabull rf	1	1	0	0
Werhas 3b	2	0	0	0	Petrocelli ss	3	2	1	1
Repoz ph	1	0	0	0	Howard c	3	0	0	0
Held 3b	3	0	0	0	Bell p	3	0	2	1
Hamilton p	1	0	0	0	**Totals**	28	3	6	2
Satriano ph	1	0	0	0					
Kelso p	0	0	0	0					
Coates p	0	0	0	0					
Morton ph	1	0	0	0					
Cimino ph	0	0	0	0					
Totals	30	2	4	2					

```
CALIFORNIA   0 0 0   0 0 0   1 0 1—2
BOSTON       0 0 0   2 0 1   0 0 x—3
```

Error: Fregosi. Double plays: California 1, Boston 1. Left on base: California 2, Boston 7. Doubles: Bell. Triples: Petrocelli. Home runs: Hall 2.

	IP	H	R	BB	SO
Hamilton (L)	5	4	2	3	2
Kelso	⅔	1	1	2	0
Coates	1⅓	1	0	0	1
Cimino	1	0	0	0	2
Bell (W)	9	4	2	1	5

Hit by pitch: By Hamilton (Conigliaro). Umpires: Valentine, Napp, Umont and Kinnamon. Time: 2:16. Attendance: 31,027.

Don Denkinger

American League : 1968–Present

The Infamous Call in 1985 World Series

"No one misses one intentionally."

WATERLOO, Ia.—"The job of an umpire is unique. Everything you do is televised and scrutinized," said Don Denkinger, the "dean" of active American League umpires.

Denkinger, 59, has been a Major League umpire for 28 years, has worked four World Series, witnessed five no-hitters and was behind the plate in one of the most exciting playoff games ever.

Yet he is probably best known for his controversial call on a play at first base in the 1985 World Series between the Kansas City Royals and St. Louis Cardinals.

The Cardinals had a three games to two edge going into game six. Charlie Liebrandt of Kansas City and Danny Cox of the Cardinals hooked up in a great pitching duel in which both teams were scoreless for seven innings.

The Cardinals pushed across a run in the eighth inning on an *RBI* single by pinch hitter Brian Harper. With relief specialist Todd Worrell on the hill in the ninth, St. Louis needed only three more outs to be the world champions.

Pinch hitter Jorge Orta led off by hitting a ground ball to Cardinal first baseman Jack Clark. Clark flipped the ball to Worrell for what looked to be the first out—but Denkinger called him safe.

"I got myself caught in a position that nobody likes," he said, recalling the play 10 years later. "I had to depend on watching the foot and listening for the sound of the ball in the glove, but the crowd was so loud I couldn't hear it.

"Sure there was an argument but I didn't realize I didn't get it right until I walked in the dressing room after the game. Commissioner Uebberoth was in there. I asked him if I got it right, and he said, 'No.'"

The Cardinals seemingly fell apart for the next few minutes. Clark let Steve Balboni's pop up drop in foul territory, after which Balboni singled. Jim

Sundberg then bunted into a force out, but both runners were able to advance when Cardinal catcher Darrell Porter let a pitch get by him for a passed ball. Then pinch hitter Dane Iorg singled home both the tying run and the game winner.

"When I found out I missed it, I was just sick. My wife and I had been invited to a cocktail party after the game, but I just went back to the hotel room. I didn't turn on the television.

"The next day, I went to the Kansas City Chiefs football game. They were playing the San Diego Chargers. I left the game about 3 o'clock so I could get ready to go to the ballpark. I still had not turned on a television set so while I felt bad about the call the night before, I had no idea of all that it had stirred up," said Denkinger.

He was behind the plate in game seven when once again, controversy prevailed. The Royals banged away and scored six runs in a stormy fifth inning in which Denkinger ejected both Cardinal manager Whitey Herzog and pitcher Joachin Andujar, who was making a rare relief appearance. The Royals went on to win the game 11-0, giving them the World Series title.

"When I had the big blowup on Sunday, I didn't like ejecting Whitey and Andujar. It was rather ugly but I didn't care. They ejected themselves, really, by their actions. Between seasons, Andujar got traded to the American League and the first time he saw me he apologized," said Denkinger.

Herzog later said Denkinger was a good umpire and that his ejection from game seven was due to frustration from the night before and the fact the Cardinals were getting blown out in this one. Herzog said he was ejected after telling Denkinger they wouldn't even be in this situation in game seven if he hadn't messed up (a loose translation) the call the night before.

How does an umpire deal with an important call he might have missed— like the play at first in the sixth game?

"You have to leave it there," said Denkinger. "It can destroy you if you let it. No one ever missed one intentionally.

"The most distressing thing about the whole situation was the anguish it caused for my family. Some disc jockey in St. Louis got hold of my home address and telephone number and gave them out over the air.

"That started an onslaught. You can't believe the calls we got. Someone threatened to burn my house down. When I drove home after the series, as I was approaching my block I noticed police cars on both sides of the street around my house because of the threats we had received. It was awful for my family," he said.

Two less obvious twists of fate had a significant impact on Denkinger's early career. The first came after he was discharged from the military service in 1959 and went to Miami to be with his girlfriend who worked for an airline there.

"One day she left a message for me that she'd left me and gone off with

Don Denkinger watches intently as a Yankee base runner tries to score ... and then emphatically gives the safe sign as both the runner and catcher watch intently.

a pilot. So here I am in Miami wondering: What am I going to do now? I saw an ad for Al Somers' umpire school and figured: Why not give it a try?

"So I went to the school, introduced myself to Mr. Somers, and he said, 'Hell, you're perfect for the school.' Later, I realized he wanted my money. That's how he made his money—by getting as many people in his school as he could. So in January 1960 I started in the school. It lasted six weeks and I did pretty well—in fact better than I knew.

"They hired six of us to go to the Alabama-Florida League. That was Class D and I stayed there a year. Then I went to the Northwest League, Class B, and was there two years. Then I moved up to Double-A, the Texas League. I signed that contract for the Texas League and three hours later, got an offer from the International League which was Triple-A.

"I tried to get out of the Double-A contract but I couldn't. I had to stay in the Texas League which was a real 'driving league.' We drove all over Texas and Oklahoma. And I stayed in that league for three years.

"In 1966, I received a contract from George Sisler, president of the International League and I worked there for the 1966 and 1967 seasons. After the second year, I was going to quit. I thought I had spent enough time in the minor leagues and that if I was ever going to move up, I would have by now," said Denkinger.

That's when the second twist of fate occurred.

"Sisler told me he thought I would be wise to stay another year. He said, 'They're going to expand the Major Leagues in 1969 and they're going to need more umpires.' So I stayed—and he was right.

"I worked the International League with Ron Luciano. One day, I got a phone call and was told that while I had done good work, the American League was offering a contract to Ron Luciano and that I should be happy for him. And I was. Then the caller said he wanted to speak to Luciano. When Luciano got on the phone, he was told that while he had done good work, the American League was offering a contract to Don Denkinger and he should be happy for him. And he was. That's how we found out we were big league umpires."

Denkinger said he and Luciano were friends but he did not approve of the flamboyant umpire's style.

"He was putting on a show out there—shooting people out like he's got a gun. That's not our style. I think it got to the point where Ron didn't really enjoy umpiring. He was kind of making fun of it with the things he did. But the fans and the media really loved it and he didn't know how to get out of it. When *NBC* offered him a job, I think he jumped at the chance," said Denkinger.

Denkinger's first Major League game was in Kansas City as part of a crew that included John Flaherty, Bob Stewart and Marty Springstead.

"It was quite an adjustment. I had never worked with a four-man crew before. My first game was at third base and I don't think I had a call.

"My first game behind the plate was in Seattle. It's a funny thing. The league doesn't want a rookie to be behind the plate in his first game in a new ballpark so I had to wait till the second game of the series. But Seattle was a new team in the league. It was a new ballpark for all of the umpires!

"Every umpire remembers his first game behind the plate. I was nervous. Seattle played Chicago and Tommy John pitched for the White Sox. But it turned out to be an easy game.

"That first year was kind of rocky. I had a lot of ejections. The ballplayers try you. They want to see what they can get away with, to see how far they can go. I was a little quick on the trigger. You have to have confidence. So you have the attitude that you're never wrong. Over time, you mellow out. You know that you're going to miss one once in a while," said Denkinger.

He said his most memorable game was the 1978 playoff game between the New York Yankees and Boston Red Sox to determine the American League East champion.

"I always marvel at that game," he said. "Both teams had won 99 games that year and yet one of them was going to go home at the end of this one. That provides intensity. It's tough for an umpire in those situations because every play is so important."

It was October 2, 1978. Boston, behind the pitching of Mike Torrez, clung to a 2-0 lead when Yankee shortstop Bucky Dent, known more for his fielding than his hitting, hammered a three-run homer over Boston's "green monster" left field wall. New York added another run that inning and one more in the eighth on a home run by Reggie Jackson. The Red Sox tried to come back but fell short, 5-4.

"Steve Palermo and I had been told four days before the end of the season that if there was a playoff, we would go to Boston to work it," said Denkinger. "We flew to Boston and went to the hotel where we had reservations and they said they had no room for us.

"We said we had reservations and they said it didn't matter. All their rooms were full. What happened was: It seemed like everyone who had a room decided to stay over because of the playoff game. So we had nowhere to stay. I had a friend who lived in Boston. I called him and we wound up sleeping on his floor the night before the game.

"I'll tell you something really interesting about that Bucky Dent home run. Just before he hit it, he fouled a ball off his foot and it hurt him. The Yankee trainer came out to look at him.

"While that was going on, [Carlton] 'Pudge' Fisk turned around and said, 'Don, have you thought about turning the lights on?' I think he thought it was starting to get a little hard to see. But I wasn't going to do something like that in the middle of an inning. And the next pitch Dent hit out of the ballpark.

"I thought for sure, especially when Boston came up, that 'Pudge' would ask again but he never did. I saw him a couple of years later and asked why he

Oakland's Billy North scores as the Dodgers' Steve Yeager awaits the throw and umpire Don Denkinger is in position to make the call in the fourth game of the 1974 World Series. Oakland won, 5–2.

didn't and he said it was just the intensity of the situation, concentrating so hard on beating the Yankees that he just forgot about the lights."

Denkinger said a playoff game like the Red Sox–Yankee contest or an outstanding individual performance by a ballplayer puts an umpire on the spot.

"You have to remind yourself to slow down. Don't get caught up in it. You have to be objective and that means always keeping the interests of both teams in mind.

"For instance, think about what happens in a no-hitter. You're going into the eighth inning and you say to yourself: This is kind of important. But you want to be fair to both sides. So you don't want many pitches on the corners."

Denkinger has had some experience with no-hitters. He has witnessed five, including perfect games by Cleveland's Len Barker and the Rangers' Kenny Rogers, and he was the plate umpire for Nolan Ryan's sixth no-hitter on June 11, 1990, pitching for the California Angels, and for Wilson Alvarez's no-hitter for the White Sox on August 11, 1991. He also was one of the umpires for another Ryan no-hitter.

The Kenny Rogers no-hitter for Texas in 1994 is a good example of the stress an umpire can feel, said Denkinger. "Billy Bean was the home plate umpire and he hadn't been in the league very long. In fact, I think he was just filling in for someone because of an illness or something like that.

"So here he is, a rookie umpire in the big leagues, and now he's behind the plate and a guy not only has a no-hitter going, but a perfect game. And the pressure of that game, of trying to make the right calls and be fair, and yet knowing a guy's got a perfect game, made him physically sick.

"When the game was over, we tried to get him to stay on the field and watch the festivities, because you know there's always a lot going on when someone throws a no-hitter ... and this was a perfect game. But he was in the umpires' room vomiting."

Denkinger has obviously been no stranger to exciting games over the years. One of the most exciting was on October 27, 1991—the seventh game of the World Series between the Minnesota Twins and the Atlanta Braves.

It was a scoreless game going into the tenth inning, with veteran Jack Morris pitching for Minnesota and reliever Alejandro Pena toiling for Atlanta. Dan Gladden led off the bottom of the tenth with a double and was sacrificed to third. Two intentional walks later, Gene Larkin stepped to the plate for Minnesota.

"As Larkin was coming up, Bobby Cox was moving all of his outfielders way in," said Denkinger. It was a situation where a long fly ball would have won the game anyway, so the outfielders were in so they could get the best possible jump on a short fly.

"I was just passing the time of day with Larkin and I said, 'If they keep bringing all of those outfielders in, even you could hit one over their heads,' which is probably something I shouldn't have said. But you know what happened? On the next pitch—Bingo. Over their heads. Twins win."

Denkinger said he had his share of arguments with Yankee manager Billy Martin over the years. "We all did. You couldn't be an umpire in the American League without having run-ins with Billy because he always wanted you to cheat for him. Always looking for the break.

"When you saw Billy off the field, he was the nicest guy you'd ever want to meet. He'd do anything for you. But on the field, he was a totally different person," he said.

Another fiery manager was Baltimore's Earl Weaver. "Earl liked to come out and argue a call, figuring if he didn't get this one, he'd get the next one. I think he really tried to work the umps so he'd get the next call. But it doesn't work that way. If an umpire thinks he missed a call, he isn't going to make up for it by missing the next one, too. There are no make-up calls," said Denkinger.

He said he's heard many complaints over the years about how slowly the game moves, that the games take too long. Part of an umpire's duties these days is to keep a game moving, said Denkinger.

"I'll tell you how you can speed up a game—get rid of the designated hitter. If you have a designated hitter, you're going to have more hitting, and if you have more hitting, it takes longer to get three outs ... and the games take longer," he said.

Denkinger said his starting pay in the Major Leagues was $10,000. The Major League umpires' standard contract for 1996 calls for a starting salary of $75,000 with top pay of $225,000 after 30 years of service. In addition, crew chiefs get an extra $7,500 and, as part of an agreement worked out years ago, all umpires get a share of the World Series pool, which means they all get an additional $20,000.

It's a pretty good living, Denkinger concedes. But it doesn't come without its aches and pains in addition to the mental and emotional stress.

"I wrenched my knee making a call at third base last year," he said. "This job takes its toll, I'll tell you that. It was much easier when I was 32."

(*Editor's Note*: Denkinger started the 1996 season, as he had for so many years, as a crew chief, working with Tim McClelland, Tim Tschada and John Shulock. In early May, barely a month into the season, the wear and tear of his profession finally caught up with him. Denkinger underwent knee surgery and was confined to crutches for six weeks. He did not return to work until spring training in 1997. It represented another instance of anonymity of umpires. Their injuries—their "disabled lists"—are not well publicized, but they exist nonetheless.)

October 2, 1978—Boston's pennant hopes Dented

NEW YORK	ab	r	h	rbi	BOSTON	ab	r	h	rbi
Rivers cf	2	1	1	0	Burlesoz ss	4	1	1	0
Blair ph-cf	1	0	1	0	Remy 2b	4	1	2	0
Munson c	5	0	1	1	Rice rf	5	0	1	1
Piniella rf	4	0	1	0	Yastrzemski lf	5	2	2	2
Jackson dh	4	1	1	1	Fisk c	3	0	1	0
Nettles 3b	4	0	0	0	Lynn cf	4	0	1	1
Chambliss 1b	4	1	1	0	Hobson dh	4	0	1	0
White lf	3	1	1	0	Scott 1b	4	0	2	0
Thompson lf	0	0	0	0	Brohamer 3b	1	0	0	0
Doyle 2b	2	0	0	0	Bailey ph	1	0	0	0
Spencer ph	1	0	0	0	Duffy 3b	0	0	0	0
Stanley 2b	1	0	0	0	Evans ph	1	0	0	0
Dent ss	4	1	1	3	Torrez p	0	0	0	0
Guidry p	0	0	0	0	Stanley p	0	0	0	0
Gossage p	0	0	0	0	Hassler p	0	0	0	0
Totals	35	5	8	5	Drago p	0	0	0	0
					Totals	36	4	11	4

NEW YORK   000   000   4 1 0—5
BOSTON   010   001   0 2 0—4

Errors: None. Left on base: New York 6, Boston 9. Doubles: Rivers, Scott, Burleson, Munson, Remy. Home runs: Yaszstremski, Dent, Jackson. Stolen bases: Rivers 2. Sacrifices: Brohamer, Remy.

	IP	H	R	BB	SO
Guidry (W)	6⅓	6	2	1	5
Gossage	2⅔	5	2	1	5
Torrez (L)	6⅔	5	4	3	4
Stanley	⅓	2	1	0	0
Hassler	1⅔	1	0	0	2
Drago	⅓	0	0	0	0

Passed ball: Munson. Umpires: Denkinger, Evans, Clark and Palermo. Time: 2:52. Attendance: 32,925

October 26, 1985 — The call that enraged Cardinal fans

ST. LOUIS	ab	r	h	rbi	KANSAS CITY	ab	r	h	rbi
O. Smith ss	3	0	0	0	L. Smith lf	4	0	1	0
McGee cf	4	0	0	0	Wilson cf	3	0	1	0
Herr 2b	4	0	0	0	Brett 3b	4	0	0	0
J. Clark 1b	4	0	0	0	White 2b	4	0	1	0
Landrum lf	4	0	1	0	Sheridan rf	3	0	1	0
Pendleton 3b	4	1	1	0	Motley ph	0	0	0	0
Cedeno rf	2	0	1	0	Orta ph	1	0	1	0
Van Slyke rf	0	0	0	0	Balboni 1b	3	0	2	0
Porter c	3	0	1	0	Concepcion pr	0	1	0	0
Cox p	2	0	0	0	Sundberg c	4	1	1	0
Harper ph	1	0	1	1	Biancalana ss	3	0	1	0
Lawless pr	0	0	0	0	McRae ph	0	0	0	0
Dayley p	0	0	0	0	Wathan pr	0	0	0	0
Worrell p	0	0	0	0	Liebrandt p	2	0	0	0
Totals	35	1	5	1	Quisenberry p	0	0	0	0
					D. Iorg ph	1	0	1	2
					Totals	37	2	10	2

```
ST. LOUIS      0 0 0    0 0 0    0 1 0 — 1
KANSAS CITY    0 0 0    0 0 0    0 0 2 — 2
```

Double plays: Kansas City 1, St. Louis 1; Left on base: St. Louis 5, Kansas City 9; Doubles: L. Smith; Sacrifice: Liebrandt

	IP	H	R	BB	SO
Cox	7	7	0	1	8
Dayley	1	0	0	0	1
Worrell (L, 0-1)	⅓	3	2	1	0
Liebrandt	7⅔	4	1	2	4
Quisenberry (W, 1-0)	1⅓	1	0	0	0

Passed ball: Porter; Time: 2:48; Attendance: 41,628

October 27, 1991—Denkinger calls the shot

ATLANTA	ab	r	h	rbi	MINNESOTA	ab	r	h	rbi
L. Smith dh	4	0	2	0	Gladden lf	5	1	3	0
Pendleton 3b	5	0	1	0	Knobloch 2b	4	0	1	0
Gant cf	4	0	0	0	Puckett cf	2	0	0	0
Justice rf	3	0	1	0	Hrbek 1b	3	0	0	0
Bream 1b	4	0	0	0	C. Davis dh	4	0	1	0
Hunter lf	4	0	1	0	J. Brown ph	0	0	0	0
Olson c	4	0	0	0	Larkin ph	1	0	1	1
Lemke 2b	4	0	1	0	Harper c	4	0	2	0
Belliard ss	2	0	1	0	Mack rf	4	0	1	0
Blauser ss	1	0	0	0	P'gliaro 3b	3	0	0	0
Totals	35	0	7	0	Gagne ss	2	0	0	0
					Bush ph	1	0	1	0
					Newman ss	0	0	0	0
					Sirrento ph	1	0	0	0
					Leius ss	0	0	0	0
					Totals	34	1	10	1

```
ATLANTA      000  000  000  0—0
MINNESOTA    000  000  000  1—1
```

Double plays: Atlanta 3, Minnesota 1. Left on base: Atlanta 8, Minnesota 12. Doubles: Pendleton, Hunter, Gladden 2. Sacrifices: Belliard, Knobloch.

	IP	H	R	BB	SO
Smoltz	7 $\frac{1}{3}$	6	0	1	4
Stanton	$\frac{2}{3}$	2	0	1	0
Pena (L, 0-1)	1 $\frac{1}{3}$	2	1	3	1
Morris (W, 2-0)	10	7	0	2	8

Hit by pitch: By Smoltz (Hrbek). Passed ball: Harper. Umpires: Denkinger (AL), Wendlestedt (NL), Coble (AL), Tata (NL), Reed (AL), Montague (NL). Time: 3:23. Attendance: 55,118.

Terry Cooney
American League: 1975-1992

Baseball's Second Most Famous Ejection

"No matter what happens in a ballgame, the
umpire has to keep control of the game."

CLOVIS, Cal.—On September 19, 1992, Terry Cooney was working
behind the plate in Detroit when Frank Tanana threw a fastball that hit him
flush on the left knee.

He never umpired another Major League game.

"Today, I can hardly walk," said Cooney, 63, revealing a little-publicized
fact about umpires: They get hurt.

"About six or seven years before that, I got hit on the left knee by a line
drive hit by Freddie Lynn. The knee was never the same. Then when I got hit
with that Tanana pitch in '92, it was over. That ended my career. I'm still working out a worker comp settlement on that … and I need a total knee replacement," he said.

But he is anything but bitter about his career. Indeed, he is quick to point
out that umpiring turned his life around from the days when he had a dead-
end job as a prison guard in California.

"When I started working for the state penal system in California in the
1960s, I was told I would catapult to the top. I started as a prison guard and
then transferred to the Sierra Conservation Center (another detention center) where I was in charge of a physical fitness program for prisoners," said
Cooney.

"When I took the tests for the sergeant's job, I got a zero on my orals. I
became very despondent. I had been told this was a job where I was going to
move up fast and now I knew it wasn't going to happen.

"One day a convict came up to me near the gym and said: 'Why don't you
leave this depressing job?' He said he had been watching *Game of the Week* on
television and they were advertising some umpire school. He said they were
looking for umpires.

"Well, I found myself quitting my state job, getting in my pickup, driving

63

to Florida and getting into the umpires' school. It was the Umpires Specialized Training Session run by Bill Kinnamon, the old American League umpire.

"Bill took a very good liking to me and that was the break I needed. I umpired in the California A League for one year. Then I went to the Texas League, which was Double-A, for one year and then to the Pacific Coast League, Triple-A, for two years. The American League bought my contract at the end of the 1974 season," he said.

On April 8, 1975, Cooney was at third base at Cleveland's Municipal Stadium in his Major League debut.

"It was pretty amazing for a first game. The Indians were playing the Yankees and it was Frank Robinson's first game as manager—the first black manager in the Major Leagues. The place was packed—over 50,000 people, and Robinson hit a home run in that game which the Indians won," he said.

Cooney may be best remembered for ejecting Boston's Roger Clemens in the fourth game of the 1990 American League playoffs between the Red Sox and Oakland.

"Willie Randolph was at bat for Oakland. Now there's a guy who had a very small strike zone. The count went to two-and-two and the next pitch was close and I called it ball three," said Cooney.

"Well, Roger was irritated. Then the next pitch was close again and I called it ball four and now he became very incensed. The whole thing was on television, of course, and Roger had his say. Then when the cameras were off him, he said some obscenities and I ejected him.

"You hate to do that, particularly in a playoff game or a World Series game. You always hope above hope that nothing like that happens. On that particular day, I think Roger was on such an emotional high that he didn't realize what he was doing," said Cooney.

Reaction at the time was fairly predictable. Clemens said he didn't do anything to warrant expulsion. Umpire crew chief Jim Evans, who was working in right field, said Clemens was trying to show up Cooney—something umpires do not tolerate. Winning pitcher Dave Stewart said he heard the whole thing and that Clemens said "a couple of magic words."

Six years after the incident, Cooney talked about criticism he's received for ejecting Clemens too quickly.

"Now I've watched tapes of that game and I've heard broadcasters say I should have given him a break. Well, an umpire works 10 to 15 years to develop his skills, to develop his style. And you have your own style. You have to keep control. No matter what happens in a ballgame, the umpire has to keep control of the game.

"That's the toughest game I ever worked because it was only the second inning when I ejected Clemens. After that, both sides were watching everything I did, every call I made very carefully.

"I've been told that's the second most famous ejection of all time. The first one, they say, happened in a game where Babe Ruth was pitching and he argued over a ball-and-strike count and bumped an umpire on the first batter of the game. He got ejected and the guy who replaced him retired the next 27 batters."

(Editor's note: Indeed he did. On June 23, 1917, Ernie Shore threw one of the most unusual perfect games in baseball history for the Red Sox against the Washington Senators in the first game of a doubleheader at Fenway Park. Ruth, the starting pitcher, walked the lead-off hitter, Ray Morgan, with the Babe arguing on most every pitch that was called a ball. On ball four, Ruth charged the plate and was immediately ejected by home plate umpire Brick Owen. Shore came in to replace Ruth. Morgan was caught stealing and Shore retired the next 26 batters.)

"I had a game in 1981 where I ejected Billy Martin ... twice. He was managing Oakland and he was hollering at me from the first pitch. Finally, I told him if he said another word about any pitch, he was going to go.

"On the very next pitch, he began hollering again and I ejected him. Then he argued some more and ran into me. And as he was leaving, he threw dirt on my back. And I ejected him again. The umpire association brought assault charges against him for that one."

Earl Weaver gave Cooney some problems over the years, too. "He's the only man in my lifetime who hit me in the face twice and got away with it. He was arguing a call and he got going, waving his arms and he hit me twice in the face. And he got away with it because what could I do? I can't hit him— or I'm done," said Cooney.

He said Kurt Bevacqua, a utility outfielder who played for several American League teams, was the league's most talkative player. "He was a constant chatterbox and, I would say, was a real character. I knew him well from my days in the Pacific Coast League. There were several fights in games I was involved in with the Coast League and it seemed like every time I was pulling guys off the pile, there, in the middle of it, would be Kurt Bevacqua," he said.

(Editor's note: Bevacqua played 15 years in the Major Leagues for eight teams—including two stints each with Kansas City and Pittsburgh. He was a utility player used at many positions in the infield and outfield, and played in more than 100 games in only two seasons. He spent the early part of his career with Cleveland, Milwaukee and Kansas City, where Cooney came in contact with him.)

Cooney said one of the funniest incidents he had as an umpire was a play involving the California Angels. "I was umpiring at second base and on a play at second, I called a guy out but I signaled him safe. Buck Rodgers, the Angels manager, came out and said: 'Terry, what did you call?' And I told him what I had done, that I had said one thing and signaled another and told him what I really meant. And the call didn't go his way and he said, 'Well, you got it right the first time.'"

Cooney said the toughest call for an umpire is often one in which the base runner is stealing. "It's because you're moving. You can't sit still and make the call.

"Your eyes are a camera out there. Just like a camera, you want to be still—not moving—so you can focus on the play. And you can't always do that when a guy is stealing because you have to move to get in position to make the call.

"The only time you ever see an umpire kick hell out of a play is when he's moving and sometimes he can't help it. I think that's what happened to [Don] Denkinger in the 1985 World Series where some people say he missed a call," said Cooney.

(*Editor's Note:* In the 1985 World Series, the St. Louis Cardinals led three games to two, and had a 1-0 lead going into the bottom of the ninth inning against the Kansas City Royals. Jorge Orta led off and was called safe at first by Denkinger on a play where television replays showed that Orta appeared to be out. The Royals wound up scoring two to win the game and then beat the Cardinals 11-0 the next night to win the series.)

"The instant replay was created to discredit umpires. What it has done is proven that we are right 95 percent of the time," said Cooney.

"Now sometimes you hear people talk about a call and they ask: Was that a make-up call? That's ridiculous. No umpire in his right mind would make a make-up call because you try to get them all right every time.

"Sometimes guys will work on you. Managers will keep on you about certain pitches, telling you you're calling them too high or whatever. And sometimes that can work on you psychologically so you might call another pitch differently. But that's different than a make-up call. That's a manager trying to affect your concentration. And in umpiring, concentration is paramount."

Cooney's only World Series was in 1981, the Yankees versus the Dodgers. "I had home plate in the third game with Fernando Valenzuela and Dave Righetti pitching," he said.

It had already been a memorable day in Los Angeles. That morning, there had been an earthquake—not a big one, just a "chandelier rattler" as newspapers described it, but an earthquake nonetheless. (Yankee coach Yogi Berra said later he didn't even feel it. "It must have bypassed me," he said.)

Cooney was looking forward to that night's pitching matchup, Righetti and Valenzuela, only the fourth time in World Series history that two rookies were the starting pitchers. (The other times: Gene Bearden of the Cleveland Indians versus Vern Bickford of the Boston Braves in 1948; Whitey Ford of the New York Yankees against Bob Miller of the Philadelphia Phillies in 1950; and Dick Hughes of the St. Louis Cardinals against Gary Waslewski of the Boston Red Sox in 1967.)

"I had seen Righetti a lot but I had no idea of what to expect from Valenzuela," said Cooney. "As it turned out, Righetti, who was a pretty good pitcher, was gone by the third inning and the other guy pitched like he'd never been in the big leagues before."

The Dodgers, down two games to none, won the game, 5-4, despite the shaky performance by Valenzuela, who went all the way but gave up four runs on nine hits, while walking seven. The Dodgers went on to win the next three games to capture the series, four games to two.

Much more had been anticipated from the 20-year-old phenom from Mexico, who won both the Cy Young and Rookie of the Year awards after a strike-shortened regular season in which he was 13-7 and led the league in starts with 25, innings pitched with 192, strikeouts with 180 and shutouts with eight.

Cooney said that 18 years of umpiring have taken a toll on his body, particularly the knee on which surgery is imminent. Yet, even in talking about the final injury, caused by the Tanana pitch in 1992, he couldn't help but admire the man who threw the pitch.

"I saw Frank Tanana and Nolan Ryan when they were both young pitchers for the Angels. And, of course, Ryan threw hard all the time. But I'll tell you something. On a given day, on a given pitch, Frank Tanana could bring it up there as hard as anybody who's ever been in the game," he said.

"I've talked to many people about my career, about how lucky I was. I started my career real late—and I wouldn't trade a day of it for anything. Walking into Major League ballparks. Seeing everything that I've seen. It was a helluva roll for 18 years.

"When I started, I made $14,000 and the per diem was $39 a day. When I retired, I was making $150,000 a year and the per diem was $215 a day.

"There are about 300 people who go to umpire school every year and less than one percent make it to the Major Leagues.

"So it's a good living for those who can make it ... but very few make it."

October 23, 1981—Valenzuela staggers to victory

NEW YORK	ab	r	h	rbi	LOS ANGELES	ab	r	h	rbi
Randolph 2b	2	0	0	0	Lopes 2b	4	1	2	0
Mumphrey cf	5	0	0	0	Russell ss	5	1	2	0
Winfield lf	3	0	0	0	Baker lf	4	0	0	0
Piniella rf	5	1	1	0	Garvey 1b	4	1	2	0
Watson 1b	4	1	2	1	Cey 3b	2	2	2	3
Cerone c	4	2	2	2	Guerrero cf-rf	3	0	1	1
Rodriguez 3b	4	0	2	0	Monday rf	2	0	1	0
Milbourne ss	2	0	2	1	(b) Thomas cf	1	0	0	0
Righetti p	1	0	0	0	Yeager c	1	0	0	0
Frazier p	1	0	0	0	(a) Scioscia c	3	0	1	0
May p	0	0	0	0	Valenzuela p	3	0	0	0
(c) Murcer	1	0	0	0	**Totals**	32	5	11	4
Davis p	0	0	0	0					
Totals	32	4	9	4					

(a) Grounded out for Yeager in third; (b) Hit into double play for Monday in seventh; (c) Bunted into double play for May in eighth.

```
NEW YORK       0 2 2   0 0 0   0 0 0—4
LOS ANGELES    3 0 0   0 2 0   0 0 0—5
```

Left on base: New York 9, Los Angeles 9. Double plays: Randolph and Watson; Milbourne, Randolph and Watson; Russell, Lopes and Garvey; Cey and Lopes. Doubles: Lopes, Cerone, Watson, Guerrero. Home runs: Cey, Watson, Cerone. Sacrifices: Righetti, Lopes.

	IP	H	R	BB	SO
Righetti	2	5	3	2	1
Frazier (L)	2	3	2	2	1
May	3	2	0	0	1
Davis	1	1	0	0	1
Valenzuela (W)	9	9	4	7	6

Hit by pitch: By Righetti (Guerrero). Umpires: Cooney (AL), Harvey (NL), Garcia (AL), Stello (NL), Barnett (AL) and Colosi (NL). Time: 3:04. Attendance: 56,236.

October 10, 1990—A quick heave-ho for Clemens

BOSTON	ab	r	h	rbi	**OAKLAND**	ab	r	h	rbi
Burks cf	4	1	1	0	R Henderson lf	3	0	1	0
Reed 2b	4	0	1	1	D Henderson cf	4	0	0	0
Boggs 3b	4	0	2	0	Canseco rf	3	0	0	0
Greenwall lf	4	0	0	0	Jennings rf	1	0	0	0
Pena c	3	0	0	0	Baines dh	3	0	1	0
Evans dh	3	0	0	0	McGee pr	0	0	0	0
Brunansky rf	3	0	0	0	Hassey ph	0	0	0	0
Quintan lb	2	0	0	0	Bl'nship pr	0	0	0	0
Rivera ss	3	0	0	0	Lansford 3b	3	1	1	0
Totals	30	1	4	1	Steinbach c	3	0	2	0
					McGuire lb	2	1	0	1
					Randolph 2b	2	1	0	0
					Gallegoss	3	0	1	2
					Totals	27	3	6	3

```
BOSTON     0 0 0   0 0 0   0 0 1—1
OAKLAND    0 3 0   0 0 0   0 0 x—3
```

Error: Greenwell. Doubleplays: Boston 2, Oakland. Left on base: Boston 3, Oakland 5. Doubles: Gallego, Burks. Stolen bases: R. Henderson, Blankenship. Sacrifice: Lansford.

	IP	H	R	BB	SO
Clemens (L)	1⅔	3	3	1	0
Bolton	2⅔	2	0	2	3
Gray	2⅔	1	0	0	2

	IP	H	R	BB	SO
Anderson	1	0	0	1	2
Stewart (W)	8	4	1	1	1
Honeycutt	1	0	0	0	0

Umpires: Cooney, Voltaggio, McCoy, Garcia, Hirschbeck, Evans. Time: 3:02. Attendance: 49,052.

Andy Olsen
National League: 1968-1981

The Longest Scoreless Game

"In umpiring, you always shoot for the angle."

ST. PETERSBURG, Fla.—When Andy Olsen announced his retirement as a Major League umpire after the 1981 baseball season, the baseball world was concerned.

"I got about 15 phone calls. People thought I was ill. I wasn't. I just wanted to have some time to enjoy the things I like to do. Like sailing. I love sailing.

"I was 50 years old. I had no responsibilities, no kids to put through school," said the bachelor who still has the accent from his days growing up in Brooklyn.

"Baseball and umpiring had given me everything I had. I found that I could retire early ... and so I did," he said.

Olsen, 65, spent almost as much time in the minor leagues—10 years— as he did in the majors, and his most memorable game actually occurred before he got to the big leagues.

Olsen was the home plate umpire in what at the time was professional baseball's longest game—an Eastern League game between Elmira, New York, and Springfield, Massachusetts, on May 8, 1965. The game went 27 innings— and the first 25 were scoreless. That is still the record for the longest scoreless game, said Olsen.

"There was a good wind blowing in, I remember that. Springfield scored a run in the top of the 26th and, this is hard to believe—Elmira got a run in the bottom of the 26th to tie it. Think of that: The two teams go scoreless for 25 innings and then they both score in the 26th!

"Elmira won the game in the bottom of the 27th. The winning run scored on a close play at the plate. There was no argument but the Springfield manager wasn't happy with the call. He said something pretty funny. He said, 'Andy, you shortened the game on us.'

"Another thing that stands out about that game. There was a perfect game in the middle of it: Elmira pitchers retired 27 batters in a row."

Andy Olsen stares into a dugout after a close play on the bases. His first "toss" in the Major Leagues was Leo Durocher.

The game is a classic—as is Olsen's memory. Elmira pitchers Dave Leonhard, Rico Delgado and Fred Beene pitched nine perfect innings, from the ninth through the 17th inning. Two years later, Leonhard began a six-year Major League career with the Baltimore Orioles. In 1968, Beene began a Major League career that lasted seven years with three teams. Elmira's shortstop, referred to in the May 9, 1965, *Elmira Sunday Telegram* as "Goldfingers" was Mark Belanger, later an outstanding shortstop for Baltimore for 18 years. The game might have ended in the 26th inning except an Elmira outfielder struck out with the winning run in scoring position. The outfielder's name: Lou Piniella, who was destined to have a stellar Major League career with the Kansas City Royals and New York Yankees. A late-inning pinch hitter for Elmira was pitcher Ed Watt, later to be a great Oriole relief pitcher. Two days before the marathon, Watt tossed his second no-hitter of the year. And Elmira's feisty little manager spent some time in a Baltimore uniform, too. Earl Weaver went on to have a Hall of Fame career as a Major League manager.

Two other notes about the ballgame: it was delayed for an hour and a half to let the field dry after a hard rain and, once started, it lasted six hours and 24 minutes.

(*Editor's note:* The Elmira-Springfield game was surpassed in total innings on June 23, 1981, when Pawtucket pushed across a run in the bottom of the 33rd inning to defeat Rochester, 3-2. The first 32 innings were played on April 18—and the finale got phenomenal attention not only because of the length of the game but because Major League players were in the midst of a 50-day strike. The Elmira-Springfield game, though, remains the longest scoreless game in history.)

The road to the majors was a long one for Olsen, a road he originally tried to take as a ballplayer.

"When I was growing up, baseball was an obsession with me," he said. "My father would take me to sandlot games and we didn't live too far from Ebbetts Field. I remember when the Dodgers won the pennant in 1941 and Leo Durocher was the manager.

"It's ironic. I remember Leo when I was a kid. Years later, he was my first ejection in the National League," said Olsen.

"When I was growing up, my desire was always to be a baseball player. I was a first baseman and later a pitcher. I had been playing in Louisiana and the Pirates bought my contract in 1950.

"I pitched for Burlington, Lincoln and then Hollywood. Branch Rickey liked what he saw in me. I was regarded as a pretty good prospect. But I developed arm trouble. I went down to play winter ball in Puerto Rico with the San Juan Senators but I couldn't pitch. My arm was hurt.

"I came to realize I couldn't cut the mustard as a pitcher but I wanted to stay in baseball," he said.

In 1959, he entered Al Somers' umpire school in Florida. "Al wasn't there very much except to show up for a lecture or two. We had Bill Kinnamon, a great umpire and a great instructor, and Lou DiMuro, who was later killed in an auto accident where he was a pedestrian," said Olsen. (Both Kinnamon and DiMuro were American League umpires.)

"I got assigned to what they call the Sophomore League in 1959. I spent three years in the Northern League and two in the Eastern League and then an unusual thing happened. I was involved in an umpire trade!

"In June of 1965, I got traded from the Eastern League to the Coast League for Dave Phillips, who I think wanted to be closer to relatives on the East Coast. I spent three and a half years in the coast league and I worked instructional leagues for several years.

"The instructional leagues are for ballplayers to sharpen their skills but I got good exposure there. I spent ten years in the minor leagues—that's a long apprenticeship. Then in September of 1968—Friday the 13th—I got called up to the National League.

"My first game was in Philadelphia. You never forget your first game. Actually it was a doubleheader. Larry Jackson was pitching for Philadelphia. He was on his way out then but he had been a terrific pitcher and I remembered him from the minor leagues.

"They always start you out on the bases. I don't remember anything in particular about the games that day except that before the first game, when we were going over the ground rules, Stan Landes kept pointing out different places in the outfield seats where Richie Allen had hit the ball.

"Now there was a ballplayer. Boy, could he hit. I know he had some problems in different places where he played but I'll tell you, he was a good guy with umpires. He never gave us any trouble," said Olsen.

Two other Phillies who came to prominence about a decade later also made a lasting impression.

"Steve Carlton was easy to work but he had a habit of balking. Tim McCarver was his catcher, you know. Carlton only wanted to work with McCarver. He actually extended McCarver's career because that's who he wanted behind the plate.

"Well, Carlton had this slow delivery with a high kick and McCarver didn't have much of an arm, in my opinion. So Carlton knew the runner was going to steal anyway so balks didn't matter to him. That's my opinion."

A pitcher who Olsen thought was hard to get a handle on was the Braves' Phil Niekro. "Tough on hitters, tough on catchers, tough on umpires," he said. "As an umpire, I really liked to wait on a pitch, but with him, you **had** to wait on it. His knuckleball danced like crazy.

"The hardest thrower I ever saw was Nolan Ryan. He could really throw, and he threw the hardest curveball, too. Nobody threw harder than Nolan Ryan."

Olsen worked the 1974 World Series, won by Oakland over the Dodgers, four games to one.

"I had the plate in the fifth game," said Olsen. And quite a game it turned out to be.

It was Thursday, October 17. Oakland had the series lead, three games to one, and had Vida Blue, 17-15 during the regular season, ready to slam the door on the Dodgers. Los Angeles countered with Don Sutton, who led the Dodger staff with a 19-9 regular season record. This was a rematch of game two in which the A's suffered their only loss by a score of 3-2.

In what turned out to be the decisive game, Oakland took the lead in the first inning when Billy North reached base on a force out, stole second and went to third when catcher Steve Yeager's throw went into center field. North scored on Sal Bando's sacrifice fly. The A's added another run in the second on Ray Fosse's home run.

The Dodgers tied the game with two runs of their own, capped by Steve Garvey's game-tying single. The game was turned over to baseball's two best bullpen specialists: Mike Marshall of the Dodgers, who set a record that still stands by appearing in 106 games during the regular season; and Rollie Fingers of the A's—destined for the Hall of Fame for his relief work with Oakland and several other clubs.

Olsen held up play for six minutes in the bottom of the seventh inning because unruly fans had thrown debris onto the field that needed to be cleared. When play resumed, Joe Rudi hit Marshall's first pitch out of the ballpark, and that was all the A's needed to win the game and the series.

Marshall, recalling the game 20 years later, didn't use the delay of the game as an excuse. "Rudi guessed right," he said. "He liked to hit to right field. I threw him a first pitch inside fastball ... and he guessed right."

Typical of impartial umpires, Olsen wasn't caught up in the excitement of the moment either when it happened or in his recollection of it. In fact his first thought was a statistic:

"The unusual thing about that series is that four out of the five games had 3-2 scores."

He was the home plate umpire on April 17, 1976, when the Cubs blew 11-run leads—twice—and Mike Schmidt hit four home runs to power the Phillies past the Cubs, 18-16, in ten innings.

"Another unbelievable game. A wild, scoring game. The wind was blowing out but none of Schmidt's home runs were flukes. He really hit the ball," said Olsen.

Olsen said he managed to stay injury-free during most of his career and has had few ill effects since he retired, a rarity for umpires. "I have a little problem with my knee from time to time," he said. "You do a lot of running over the years. Making pivots on wet fields can be tough. And all that crouching behind the plate for all those years. It isn't easy. But I wouldn't trade it. I feel privileged."

He said the toughest call for an umpire is the half-swing. "The reason is the angle. You know the best angle on anything like that is to the side. That's why the camera always gets it better.

"It's the same way on the bases, too. I remember in the old days, in the minors, working as part of a two-man crew. Sometimes you'd have to run right with the runner to call a play and it can be a tough call when a guy is sliding into second base. It's actually possible to get too close so the play blocks your view. You can't get too close," said Olsen. "In umpiring, you always shoot for the angle. That's the key."

May 8, 1965—Baseball's longest scoreless game

SPRINGFIELD	ab	r	h	ELMIRA	ab	r	h
Edmonson 2b	9	0	0	Belanger ss	9	0	1
E'berger 3b	10	0	2	Scroggs cf	10	1	2
Taylor lf	8	0	2	Stone rf	10	0	1
McClain rf	10	0	1	Rouse 1b	10	0	1
Linares rf	11	0	1	Haney c	11	0	2
Engbers 1b	10	0	0	Riddle lf	8	1	5
Torres ss	8	0	1	Peters 3b	8	0	1
Sommers c	8	1	0	Nichols 2b	9	0	1
Arruda p	3	0	0	Leonhard p	3	0	1
Juarez ph	1	0	0	Hickerson ph	1	0	0
Wade p	1	0	0	Delgado p	1	0	0
Reinoso p	1	0	0	McGuire ph	1	0	0
Turnbull p	3	0	1	Martinez ph	1	0	0
Totals	83	1	8	Piniella pr	5	0	0
				Beene p	2	0	0
				Watt ph	1	0	0
				Totals	85	2	14

```
SPGFLD   000   000   000   000   000   000   000   000 010—1
ELMIRA   000   000   000   000   000   000   000   000 011—2
```

Errors: Engbers 2, Beene. RBI: Eichelberger, Nichols, Haney. Doubleplays: Springfield 3, Elmira 1. Left on base: Springfield 14, Elmira 21. Doubles: Riddle, Peters, Scroggs. Stolen base: Stone. Sacrifice: Stone, Edmonson, Leonhard, Belanger, Peters, Haney. Sacrifice fly: Nichols.

	IP	H	R	BB	SO
Arruda	11	7	0	4	5
Wade	3 ⅔	0	0	2	1
Reinoso	2 ⅓	1	0	0	3
Turnbull (L)	9 ⅓	6	2	5	5
Leonhard	12	5	0	4	7
Delgado	3	0	0	0	2
Beene (W)	12	4	1	3	6

Hit by pitch: By Arruda (Peters). Wild pitch: Leonhard, Turnbull. Passed ball: Sommers. Time: 6:24. Attendance: 384

Oct. 17, 1974—A game delay, a pitch, a home run

LOS ANGELES	ab	r	h	rbi	OAKLAND	ab	r	h	rbi
Lopes 2b	2	1	0	0	Campana's ss	4	0	2	0
Buckner lf	3	0	1	0	North cf	4	1	0	0
Wynn cf	2	0	0	1	Bando 3b	3	0	0	1
Garvey 1b	4	0	1	1	Jackson rf	2	0	0	0
Ferguson rf	4	0	1	0	Rudi 1b-lf	3	1	2	1
Cey 3b	3	0	1	0	Washington lf	3	0	1	0
Russell ss	3	0	0	0	Fingers p	0	0	0	0
(b) Crawford	1	0	0	0	Fosse c	3	1	1	1
Yeager c	2	0	0	0	Green 2b	2	0	0	0
(c) Joshua	1	0	0	0	Blue p	2	0	0	0
Sutton p	1	0	0	0	Odom p	0	0	0	0
(a) Paciorek	1	1	1	0	Tenace 1b	1	0	0	0
Marshall p	0	0	0	0	**Totals**	28	3	6	3
Totals	27	2	5	2					

(a) Doubled for Sutton in sixth. (b) Popped out for Russell in ninth. (c) Grounded out for Yeager in ninth.

```
LOS ANGELES  0 0 0   0 0 2   0 0 0—2
OAKLAND      1 1 0   0 0 0   1 0 x—3
```

Double: Paciorek. Home runs: Fosse, Rudi. Stolen bases: North, Campaneris. Sacrifice: Buckner. Sacrifice fly: Bando, Wynn. Double plays: Campaneris, Green and Rudi. Left on base: Los Angeles 6, Oakland 3.

	IP	H	R	BB	SO
Sutton	5	4	2	1	3
Marshall (L)	3	2	1	0	4
Blue	6⅔	4	2	5	4
Odom (W)	⅓	0	0	0	0
Fingers	2	1	0	1	0

Umpires: Olsen (NL), Luciano (AL), Gorman (NL), Kunkel (AL), Harvey (NL), Denkinger (AL). Time: 2:23. Attendance: 49,347.

Marty Springstead
American League, 1966–1985

Manager Forces Forfeited Game

It used to be an 8-0 game was a breeze ... Now
you got guys stealin' bases and trying to stretch
singles into doubles, all because of incentive clauses."

NEW YORK—It had not been an easy week for Marty Springstead.

"I got seven guys out with injuries," said the supervisor of American League umpires. "It isn't easy finding replacements and getting them where they need to go.

"The league is so spread out—from Toronto to California to Texas to Boston. It isn't like we're all sittin' around together in a room and I say, 'All right, you go upstairs and you go downstairs.' No, we're talkin' about gettin' men from one end of the country to another, makin' the right plane connections, gettin' the hotel reservations. I'll tell ya somethin'—you try gettin' a hotel room in Chicago in August when the Democratic convention is going on. They don't care that you're an umpire."

Springstead was an American League umpire for 20 years and became supervisor of umpires when Dick Butler stepped down. "I didn't retire, Dick Butler did," said Springstead. "If he hadn't retired, I'd still be umpiring."

Springstead, a native New Yorker, has what people in the rest of the country would describe as a "New Yawk" accent, and he talks quickly on this day, interrupted twice by telephone calls from the men he supervises, the men he calls "my guys."

It is Friday, there is a full schedule of games, but tonight, just like last night, some will have only three umpires. Not all the travel connections panned out.

"When I was young, I played semi-pro ball in the New York area. I began to realize the umpires were making more money than I was, and I decided to give it a try," said Springstead.

"I was umpiring a game in Patterson, New Jersey, one day when a guy came up to me and said, 'You're a pretty good umpire. You ought to think about

77

going to umpire school.' At the time, I didn't even know there was such a thing as umpire school.

"But I looked into it and went to Al Somers' umpire school. It wasn't like you had to try out or anything. You didn't have to apply. They'd take just about anybody. That didn't mean you were going to make it, of course, but at least you were in.

"So I went through the school and then my father passed away. I was an only child and I had to go back home and take care of some things. That was in 1959. In 1960, I got assigned to the Northern League, Class C, and then I got drafted. Back in those days, you know, they had the military draft—and they got me—and I went to Fort Hood, Texas, for two years, and I wound up playin' ball there.

"When I got out of the service, I was goin' back to the Northern League, and four days before the season started, I got a call askin' me to go to the Southern League. That was a real break for me because that was Double A ball—strictly a matter of being in the right place at the right time.

"I spent three years there and then in 1966, the American League bought my contract. I went up to the American League with Emmett Ashford and Jerry Neudecker," said Springstead.

"My first game was in Fenway Park. I was at third base. I had one play there that was a real banger—and nobody yelled at me or anything. And I thought: 'Boy, this is pretty easy.' Well, it didn't stay that way for long.

"When you look back at your career, you look at highlights, milestones. Umpires don't have favorite games. To an umpire, a ballgame's a ballgame. But you do have milestones. For me, a real milestone was my first game in Yankee Stadium.

"I grew up in New York, and my Dad used to take me to the ballgame—to the old Polo Grounds where the Giants played, and of course to Yankee Stadium. So now, here I am, workin' the plate at Yankee Stadium. I had been there so many times with my Dad, sittin' in the stands lookin' down on the field. And now I'm down on the field, lookin' up at all the people. Yeah, that's a highlight.

"Umpires have numbers. We didn't wear 'em in those days but they were on scorecards to help identify us. Well, the American League had 20 umpires back then; there was no number 13. So I was number 21.

"The old umpire Ed Runge was part of our crew and he saw that I was number 21 and he reminded me that there were only 20 umpires. He laughed and said: 'Do you suppose they're tryin' to tell you something?'

"All-Star games, playoff games and World Series games are all highlights, too, I suppose. My first World Series was in '73—Oakland and the Mets, Willie Mays' last games. I got the plate in game one and game seven.

"You talk about reachin' out and grabbin' something—the seventh game of a World Series has some pressure to it. As you get more experience you get used to it. But let me tell you somethin'. By that time you've gone through about 30 games in spring training, 162 games during the regular season, the league playoffs and now you're down to the seventh game of the World Series.

"It's October. You've been involved in over 200 games since March and now it's down to one game, the only game in town, and everyone from Alvin, Texas, to California is watching. Brother, that's pressure."

Oakland helped take the pressure off by scoring four runs in the third inning—including home runs by Bert Campaneris and Reggie Jackson. Amazingly, they were Oakland's first home runs of the series. The A's added a run in the fifth and held on as the Mets scored runs in the sixth and the ninth. The game and series ended when Wayne Garrett, representing the tying run, popped out to make Oakland a 5-2 winner.

"The second game of that '73 Series seemed like the longest game I'd ever been involved in. Something like five hours. That's the thing I remember about that game."

The Mets beat Oakland 10-7 in a game that lasted four hours and 13 minutes. Mays, 42, entered the game in the ninth inning as a pinch hitter and then went out to play center field in the bottom of the ninth. Deron Johnson hit a fly ball to center, the kind Mays had caught a thousand times over his 22-year-career. But he misplayed this one and wound up sprawled on the ground in center field, symbolizing a career that was crawling to an end.

Johnson's hit, scored as a double, was a key factor in the A's two-run rally to tie the game at 6-6. It stayed that way until the Mets rallied in the 12th inning. With runners on first and third and two out, Mays laced a single to center to drive in a run and keep the inning alive. Before it was over, four Met runners crossed the plate. It was the last hit of Mays' career.

Springstead also worked the 1978 World Series in which the New York Yankees won four straight games after the Los Angeles Dodgers had won the first two; and the 1983 World Series between the Baltimore Orioles and the Philadelphia Phillies. "I had home plate in games one and seven of that one, too, but thank God the Orioles took care of 'em in five games," he said.

Baltimore manager Earl Weaver provided Springstead with perhaps the most controversial ruling of his career. "Earl was a character but there were a lot of colorful managers in my time—Earl, Billy Martin, Eddie Stanky, Ralph Houk, they could all give it to you," he said.

On September 15, 1977, Baltimore was locked in a tight race with the Yankees with two weeks to go in the season when the Orioles went to Toronto to face the fledgling Blue Jays, who were in their first American League season.

Weaver noticed a tarpaulin in the Toronto bullpen and asked that it be removed. Springstead, who was the crew chief that night, recalls what happened after that.

"Earl wanted the tarp removed. It wasn't in the way or anything so we said 'No. Let's go.' So Earl refused to put his team on the field. Now there were only about ten games left in the season and the Orioles were about a game-and-a-half out of first place at the time. So it's a big ballgame. And Earl's got his team in the dugout and they won't come out.

"I went over to him and I said, 'We got a ballgame to play and how can I play it with only one team on the field?' And he still refused to take the field. And I said, 'Earl, what do you want me to do, choose up sides?' Finally, I had no choice. The game was forfeited to the Blue Jays. I hated to do it, with the pennant race and all."

Springstead invoked Rule 4:15 (a) of Major League rules, which gives the umpire the right to forfeit a game if one of the teams refuses to take the field within five minutes after the umpire says to start play.

Baltimore finished two-and-a-half games behind the first-place Yankees.

Springstead said today's players and managers approach the game much differently than when he first got into umpiring. "There's a different breed of cat now. Screamin' and hollerin' and kickin' dirt—that's all kind of passé now. They used to do it from the get-go. They hardly do it at all anymore.

"I think there's a couple of reasons. Every game played is televised now, maybe not all over, but televised some place. So there's a lot more people watching and that puts more pressure on everybody.

"And incentive clauses have changed everything. You gotta stay in the game or you don't get the numbers you need for those incentives. So everyone's fighting for everything they can get for those individual numbers.

"It used to be an 8-0 game was a breeze, particularly in the late innings. Now you got guys stealin' bases and trying to stretch singles into doubles, all because of incentive clauses. It's a different game now," said Springstead.

"It's a terrific grind for umpires," he said. "Hey, we wouldn't do it if we didn't love it but it's not an easy haul. There's no goin' home, you know. We don't get home games like the players do. For us, we're in California for three days, then have to be in Chicago the following afternoon and stay there for two days and then be in Cleveland the following night.

"The job itself is sometimes the best part of it—the actual workin' on the field. It's everything in between that can get to you. The travel. The hotels. The lack of rest. Weather delays that force you to change all of your plans, all of your scheduling. A lot of things enter into it."

Springstead said as supervisor of umpires, his main responsibility is to make sure enough umpires are on the field every night for every game.

"I'm the buffer between the umpires and all the people they have to deal with. And I answer all the hate mail," he said, laughing once again.

"I'm the guy who assigns the umpires and makes sure every game is covered. And that means scouting the Triple A guys so we know who we want to bring up in case something happens. There's a lot to it and sometimes you have to make do, like last night where we worked three games with only three umpires." (The record shows that on Thursday, June 20, 1996, Baltimore beat

Texas 3-2, California defeated Milwaukee 10-3 and Seattle beat Chicago 8-5—all games in which there were only three umpires.)

The phone rings again, and Springstead apologizes and takes the call from one of his "guys." He's going to be a while. There are scheduling problems to work out.

Like he said: It's not as easy as: "You go upstairs and you go downstairs."

October 21, 1973—Game 7—"Brother, that's pressure."

NEW YORK	ab	r	h	rbi	OAKLAND	ab	r	h	rbi
Garrett 3b	5	0	0	0	Campaneris ss	4	2	3	2
Milan 2b	4	1	1	0	Rudi lf	3	1	2	1
Staub rf	4	0	2	1	Bando 3b	4	0	0	0
Jones lf	3	0	0	0	Jackson cf-rf	4	1	1	2
Milner 1b	3	1	0	0	Tenace c-1b	3	0	0	0
Grote c	4	0	1	0	Alou rf	1	0	0	0
Hahn cf	4	0	3	0	(a) Dav'llo cf	3	0	0	0
Harrelson ss	4	0	0	0	Johnson 1b	3	0	0	0
Matlack p	1	0	0	0	Fosse c	1	0	1	0
Parker p	1	0	0	0	Green 2b	4	0	0	0
(b) B'champ	1	0	0	0	Holtzman p	2	1	1	0
Sadecki p	0	0	0	0	Fingers p	1	0	1	0
(c) Boswell	1	0	1	0	Knowles p	0	0	0	0
Stone p	0	0	0	0	**Totals**	33	5	9	5
(d) Kranep'l	1	0	0	0					
(e) Mart'nez	0	0	0	0					
Totals	35	2	8	2					

(a) Flied out for Alou in third. (b) Struck out for Parker in fifth. (c) Singled for Sadecki in seventh. (d) Safe on error for Stone in ninth. (e) Ran for Kranepool in ninth.

```
NEW YORK   0 0 0   0 0 1   0 0 1—2
OAKLAND    0 0 4   0 1 0   0 0 x—5
```

Doubles: Holtzman, Milan, Staub. Home runs: Campaneris, Jackson. Double plays: Bando, Campaneris and Green. Left on base: New York 8, Oakland 6.

	IP	H	R	BB	SO
Holtzman (W)	5 ⅓	5	1	1	4
Fingers	3 ⅓	3	1	1	2
Knowles	⅓	0	0	0	0
Matlack (L)	2 ⅔	4	4	1	3
Parker	1 ⅓	0	0	1	1
Sadecki	2	2	1	0	1
Stone	2	3	0	0	3

Umpires: Springstead (AL), Donatelli (NL), Neudecker (AL), Pryor (NL), Goetz (AL), Wendelstedt (NL). Time: 2:37. Attendance: 49,333.

Doug Harvey
National League: 1962–1992

The Kirk Gibson Home Run

"When he hit it, I said to myself: 'Either
go out of the park or somebody catch
it, 'cause I don't want extra innings.'"

SPRINGVILLE, Cal.—Doug Harvey would be the first to tell you he
beat the odds.

He became one of the National League's most respected umpires—and
had one of the league's longest tenures even though:
* He never went to umpiring school; and
* He jumped to the Major Leagues after only one year in Triple A and
three years altogether in the minors.

But Harvey, 65, is not bashful about what helped him succeed. "I never
let up. Even in the minor leagues, I always gave it my best," he said. "Umpiring was my life."

As a teenager (when the first signs of his trademark silver-white hair
began to show), he made a decision that would shape the rest of his life.

"When I was about 16, I was playing basketball and I didn't like the way
the refs were handling the game," said Harvey. "I decided to get into refereeing. I was a basketball ref for 27 years, a football referee for 22 years and a
baseball umpire for 47 years.

"I was the last of the umpires in the National League who didn't go to
school. I was fortunate but I also worked hard," he said.

"I umpired in the California State League, Class C, for three years, from
1958 to 1960. Then I went to the Pacific Coast League in '61 and to the majors
in '62. I'm the only umpire ever to go from C ball to one year in Triple A and
then be in the Major Leagues."

Harvey said when you're umpiring in the minors, you have to get a break;
somebody has to notice you. He remembers well the break he got.

"When I was in C ball, I worked a lot of instructional league games. I
remember working games in Phoenix when Lou Brock used to wear a helmet

in the outfield because he was so bad on fly balls. Boog Powell played down there and so did Jim Palmer.

"A lot of umpires just went through the motions down there because it was basically a league for ballplayers to improve their skills. But I gave it everything I had because I didn't know how to do it any other way. That's just Doug Harvey.

"Well, one day a man watching the game told my wife, 'Tell your husband he's too good to be in C Ball.' A week later, I was signed by the Pacific Coast League. The man who had talked to my wife was Pants Rowland, vice president of the Chicago Cubs.

"My first major league game was April 10, 1962. Everybody remembers their first game. I was at third base in Dodger Stadium—the first game ever played in Dodger Stadium. I don't remember anything in particular about the game except the excitement of being there. Imagine—a guy who was in Class C ball two years before. Now, here I am in Dodger Stadium in front of thousands of people.

"About the sixth inning, the great Al Barlick, my crew chief, walked down to third base and said, 'Well, what do you think of this joint?' and I said, 'You could stack a lot of hay in here.' That's the old California farmer coming out in me."

Harvey was involved in some classic games in his career, but he treated them all as part of the job. Even in retirement, he had difficulty pinpointing his most exciting games—because he was never at the ballpark as a fan. He was working.

He was the home plate umpire in the first game of the 1988 World Series when Kirk Gibson hit one of the most dramatic home runs in World Series history.

The Los Angeles Dodgers were playing the Oakland A's. Jose Canseco hit a grand-slam home run in the second inning to put the A's up 4-2 and they hung on to a 4-3 lead going into the bottom of the ninth inning.

To no one's surprise, A's manager Tony LaRussa brought in his bullpen ace, Dennis Eckersley, to finish off the Dodgers. Eckersley, the premiere short relief pitcher in the Major Leagues, rarely allowed base runners and he kept true to form when he retired the first two Dodgers.

Then, a rarity: Dodger Mike Davis worked Eckersley for a walk. (During the regular season, Eckersley walked just 11 batters in 73 innings—an average of 1.4 walks per every nine innings.)

Dodger manager Tom Lasorda called on Gibson to pinch hit. The left-handed slugger was a major reason the Dodgers were even in the World Series—but ligament damage in his left knee forced him out of the seventh game of the playoffs against the Mets and he was questionable at best for the World Series.

Gibson hobbled up to the plate in obvious pain and winced on every pitch. He worked the count to two-and-two as he fouled off four consecutive pitches. For the crowd, it was sheer drama. For Gibson, it was sheer agony.

On the next pitch, ball three, Davis stole second. LaRussa now had the option of walking Gibson to set up a force play. But that would have put the potential winning run on first. Besides—there were two outs, and Eckersley, the best relief pitcher in baseball who had 45 saves during the regular season, was on the mound. And a man who could hardly walk was in the batter's box with two strikes on him.

Eckersley fired, Gibson swung—and drove the ball into the right-field seats. It was the first final inning, come-from-behind, game-winning homer in World Series history.

Gibson said after the game that despite his pain, "I could suck it up for one AB."

From behind the plate, Harvey's reaction was not that of a man caught up in the moment.

"When he hit it, I said to myself: 'Either go out of the park or somebody catch it 'cause I don't want extra innings,'" he recalled eight years later.

"You don't get wrapped up in the excitement of something like that because that's just the way the game of baseball is. We see it every day," said Harvey.

"We have to concentrate on keeping the game level and even. Like if someone's got a no-hitter going, for example. You can't root. That's not fair to the other team. And you might change your strike zone."

Harvey was behind the plate in the fifth game of 1968 World Series between the Detroit Tigers and St. Louis Cardinals. "I made a call that a lot of people have said was a turning point in the series," he said.

The Cardinals were up, three games to one. Bob Gibson, who won 22 games in the regular season and finished with a 1.12 earned run average, matched up twice against the Tigers' 31-game winner, Dennis McLain, and was the victor both times. In the first game, Gibson set a single-game World Series record with 17 strikeouts.

The Cardinals went into game five needing only one more victory to become World Series champions. Nelson Briles started for the Cardinals. Detroit countered with lefthander Mickey Lolich, always in the shadows of McLain during the regular season but who was the winner in game two, the Tigers' only series victory.

In the first inning, Lou Brock doubled, Curt Flood singled and Orlando Cepeda homered—and the Cardinals had a 3-0 lead before Detroit had even batted.

It stayed that way until the bottom of the fourth, when the Tigers parlayed triples by Mickey Stanley and Willie Horton into two runs.

Then, in the fifth inning, Brock doubled and Julian Javier followed with a single to left. Brock rounded third and cruised home but did not touch the plate before being tagged by Tiger catcher Bill Freehan on an extremely close play. Horton, the Tiger left fielder, had made a perfect throw that apparently surprised Brock.

"I called Lou Brock out at the plate. He crossed home plate without touching it," said Harvey. "He came in standing up. He should have slid. They say it was a turning point of the series."

The Tigers went on to win that game, 5-3, came back with McLain to win 13-1 in game six and finished the Cardinals off with a 4-1 win in game seven with Lolich winning for the third time.

Harvey said one oddity of his long career was that he never called a no-hitter. "Never had one behind the plate and was never even on the field for one," he said.

"I worked the plate once when Doug Drabek of Pittsburgh took a no-hitter into the ninth inning and lost it and I was on the field when Tom Seaver had a perfect game for 8⅔ innings and then Jimmy Qualls of the Cubs hit a little flare for a hit to break it up. That's as close as I ever came. Once when I took some days off for vacation, my crew had a no-hitter—but I never had one—not in 47 years of umpiring."

Harvey said he believes he came into the National League at a great time, "when some of the greatest stars were blossoming.

"I came in at the end of Stan Musial's career and at the start of Pete Rose's. And there was Mays and Aaron and Clemente. And Spahn and Koufax and Drysdale.

"Wilie Mays had a great attitude. I only saw Willie get mad twice," said Harvey. "Once he slid into third on a close play and Jocko Conlan called him out. Willie got up and said, 'Oh, no, Jocko' and bumped up against him and when he realized what he did, he said, 'Oh, my.' That was an outburst for Willie.

"Another time I called him out on a close play at first base. He had stumbled coming into first and when he saw I called him out he came up to me and I said, 'Willie, you're too close' and I think he agreed. He backed off. He was truly the best all-around ballplayer I ever saw. He could do anything," said Harvey.

"Now Pete Rose was one of the biggest characters who ever came down the runway. There was a fire in him.

"I remember seeing him in the spring of 1963. He was a rookie but even then he had that fire. But one day he came out to second base and didn't say anything. He didn't even say hello.

"I said, 'What's wrong, Pete?' He said, 'I've looked at this Cincinnati infield. I'm not going to make this ballclub.'

"I said, 'Pete, don't worry about that. You're going to make the team and you're going to be here a long time.' And I was right."

Harvey said the travel schedule can be grueling for an umpire—and it's far different than it is for players. "There's no home and away games for umpires. There are no homestands for us. If we sleep in our own beds 12 nights in a season, it's been a good year."

When asked what the toughest call is for an umpire, his answer was so quick he started to speak before the questioner had finished asking.

"The sweep tag. The guy is stealing second and the catcher throws the ball on the first base side. You get the fielder's body between you and the runner. That is absolutely the toughest call in baseball because you don't have the position, the angle you need," said Harvey.

Harvey probably never had a more unusual call than one he made in a game between the San Diego Padres and Pittsburgh Pirates—but it is a call that exemplifies his knowledge of the rules and his control over a ballgame.

Padres broadcaster Jerry Coleman recalls how when the lineup cards were submitted before the game, the name of Pittsburgh outfielder Willie Stargell was accidentally written in both the fourth spot and the sixth spot in the batting order.

Padre manager Alvin Dark noticed the mistake but didn't say anything until Stargell, batting fourth, doubled, and the sixth batter came to the plate—the man also listed as Stargell on the lineup card.

Dark protested to Harvey behind the plate, saying both players couldn't be Stargell. Harvey told Dark he didn't care who the batter was and told the manager to go sit down.

The next day, Dark questioned Harvey about the call and Harvey told him to go check the rules. In this case, the sixth batter in the lineup was not Stargell, as listed, but he was not batting out of turn. He was just batting with a different name than his own. Major league baseball rules say that when something happens on the field that is not covered by any rule, the umpire can do whatever he deems best to move the game along.

Harvey applied an obscure rule to a most unusual set of circumstances and maintained control of the ballgame.

"I go out three times a year to an umpiring school. Several young Major League umpires work there and I help out. More than anything else, we teach position and timing. Getting the right angle on a play is important. If you get the proper position, you'll get the right angle," he said.

Harvey said he enjoys going to the umpiring schools because he knows what kind of life is ahead for those who go on from the school.

"I used to have a sign in my locker that said, 'When I'm right no one remembers. When I'm wrong, no one forgets.'

"That's why I go to the umpiring school. I want to make life easier for umpires. For me, umpiring was more than a job. It was a religion. I gave it everything I had."

He said he will never forget the help he received from veteran umpires when he was young. "The guys who taught me in the Major Leagues are Al

Barlick, Jocko Conlan and Shag Crawford. I owe an awful lot to them," he said.

Harvey is a proud, confident man and perhaps one incident that happened nearly 40 years ago best shows the zeal and dedication he brought to the game.

"One time in the instructional league, Ray Ripplemeyer, pitching coach of the Philadelphia Phillies, came up to me and said, 'You're a good umpire. But if you want to make it to the Major Leagues, you better dye your hair and get rid of that chewing tobacco.'

"I told him, 'If they don't want a gray-haired, tobacco-chewing umpire, then I guess they don't want me," said Harvey, who said he got his first gray hair when he was 13 years old.

"A few years later, I was in the Major Leagues, umpiring at first base in a game against the Phillies. I went over to the dugout in front of Ripplemeyer, spit tobacco juice on his foot and said: 'Well, I made it.'"

Indeed, Doug Harvey made it ... for 31 years in the National League.

October 7, 1968—Brock is out at the plate!

ST. LOUIS	ab	r	h	rbi	DETROIT	ab	r	h	rbi
Brock lf	5	1	3	0	McAuliffe 2b	4	1	1	0
Javier 2b	4	0	2	0	Stanley ss-cf	3	2	1	0
Flood cf	4	1	1	1	Kaline rf	4	0	2	2
Cepeda 1b	4	1	1	2	Cash 1b	2	0	2	2
Shannon 3b	4	0	0	0	Horton lf	4	1	1	0
McCarver c	3	0	1	0	Oyler ss	0	0	0	0
Davis rf	3	0	0	0	Northrup cf-lf	3	0	1	1
(a) Gagliano	0	0	0	0	Freehan c	4	0	0	0
Maxvill ss	3	0	0	0	Wert 3b	3	0	0	0
(b) Spiezio	1	0	1	0	Lolich p	4	1	1	0
(c) Schofield	0	0	0	0	**Totals**	31	5	9	5
Briles p	2	0	0	0					
Hoerner p	0	0	0	0					
Willis p	0	0	0	0					
(d) Maris	1	0	0	0					
Totals	35	3	9	0					

(a) Flied out for Davis in ninth; (b) Singled for Maxvill in ninth; (c) Ran for Spiezio in ninth; (d) Struck out for Willis in ninth.

ST. LOUIS   3 0 0   0 0 0   0 0 0—3
DETROIT   0 0 0   2 0 0   2 0 x—5

Doubles: Brock, 2. Triples: Stanley, Horton. Home runs: Cepeda. Stolen bases: Flood. Sacrifice fly: Cash. Double plays: Shannon, Javier and Cepeda. Left on base: St. Louis 7, Detroit 7.

	IP	H	R	BB	SO
Briles	6 ⅓	6	3	3	5
Hoerner (L)	0	3	2	1	1
Willis	1 ⅔	0	0	0	1
Lolich (W)	9	9	3	1	8

Hit by pitch: By Lolich (Briles). Umpires: Harvey (NL), Haller (AL), Gorman (NL), Honochick (AL), Landes (NL), Kinnamon (AL). Time: 2:43. Attendance: 53,634.

October 15, 1988—Gimpy Gibson hits the game-winner

OAKLAND	ab	r	h	rbi	LOS ANGELES	ab	r	h	rbi
Langford 3b	4	0	1	0	Sax 2b	3	1	1	0
Henderson cf	5	0	2	0	Stubbs 1b	4	0	0	0
Canseco rf	4	1	1	4	Hatcher lf	3	1	1	2
Parker lf	2	0	0	0	Marshall rf	4	1	1	0
Javier lf	1	0	1	0	Shelby cf	4	0	1	0
McGuire 1b	3	0	0	0	Scioscia c	4	0	1	1
Steinbach c	4	0	1	0	Hamilton 3b	4	0	0	0
Hassey c	0	0	0	0	Griffin ss	2	0	1	0
Hubbard 2b	4	1	2	0	M. Davis ph	0	1	0	0
Weiss ss	4	0	0	0	Belcher p	0	0	0	0
Stewart p	3	1	0	0	Heep ph	1	0	0	0
Eckersley p	0	0	0	0	Leary p	0	0	0	0
Totals	34	4	7	4	Woodson ph	1	0	0	0
					Horton p	0	0	0	0
					Gonzales ph	1	0	0	0
					Pena p	0	0	0	0
					Gibson ph	1	1	1	2
					Totals	32	5	7	5

OAKLAND   0 4 0   0 0 0   0 0 0—4
LOS ANGELES   2 0 0   0 0 1   0 0 2—5

Double plays: Oakland 1. Left on base: Oakland 10, Los Angeles 5. Doubles: Henderson. Home runs: Hatcher, Canseco, Gibson. Stolen base: Canseco, Sax, M. Davis.

	IP	H	R	BB	SO
Stewart	8	6	3	3	2
Eckersley (L)	⅔	1	2	1	1
Belcher	2	3	4	4	3
Leary	2	3	0	1	3
Horton	2	0	0	0	0
Pena (W)	2	1	0	0	3

Hit by pitch: By Belcher (Canseco). By Stewart (Sax). Balk: Stewart. Umpires: Harvey (NL), Merrill (AL), Froemming (NL), Cousins (AL), Crawford (NL), McCoy (AL). Time: 3:04. Attendance: 55,983.

W. Kenneth Burkhart
National League: 1957–1973

Strange Play in 1970 World Series

"That was quite a play ... and I was on my behind."

KNOXVILLE, Tenn.—It had been quite a year in Cincinnati. The Reds' new ballpark, Riverfront Stadium, was baseball's newest palace. In July, the All-Star game was played there and it ended when Cincinnati's Pete Rose bowled over Cleveland catcher Ray Fosse to score the winning run.

The Reds went on to win the National League pennant. On October 10, 1970, the Reds faced the Baltimore Orioles in the first World Series game ever played at Riverfront. It was also the first World Series game ever played on artificial turf.

Ken Burkhart was umpiring behind the plate and he will never forget what happened there in the sixth inning—nor will thousands of Cincinnati fans.

World Series games had their share of pressures, said Burkhart, now 80 years old, "because you feel like you have to work hard and get everything right." It is the World Series, after all.

The ballgame was a good one. The Reds scored a run in the bottom of the first inning off Jim Palmer and added two more in the third. The Orioles fought back to tie it with two runs in the fourth inning and another in the fifth.

In the bottom of the sixth, one of the strangest plays in World Series history occurred—and Burkhart was right in the middle of it.

The Reds threatened to break the 3-3 tie when Ty Cline came to the plate as a pinch hitter for shortstop Woody Woodward. Bernie Carbo was on third, Tommy Helms was on first and there was one out.

Cline hit a chopper that bounced high in front of the plate. Burkhart, the home plate umpire, threw off his mask, ran around to straddle the third baseline and signaled that it was a fair ball.

Twenty-six years later, Burkhart picked up the story.

"The ball was 10 or 15 feet in the air. I'm watching it when I hear Jim Palmer yelling, 'Here he comes, here he comes' and I realize Carbo's trying to score.

"Well, Carbo comes in and as he slides, he hooks his feet around mine, and I land right on my behind. Now, you see, here's a man trying to score to break a tie in the World Series ... and I'm on my behind.

"Well, I call Carbo out and there's a big argument. Sparky Anderson comes out and says, 'Why did you call him out?' and I said, 'Because he was out, Sparky, and I don't want you to talk about this too long.' And Sparky goes back to the dugout saying, 'I want to see a replay.'

"The next day, I saw the replay. Elrod Hendricks was the Baltimore catcher and he tagged Carbo, all right. He tagged him with his glove but the ball was in his other hand. And when Carbo slid in, he missed the plate. Later, someone asked Casey Stengel what he thought about the play and old Casey said, 'It was a dead heat: Carbo missed the plate, Hendricks missed the tag and Burkhart missed the call.' That was quite a play ... and I was on my behind."

Burkhart was a promising pitcher in the National League when his career was cut short by injuries. In 1945, he had a 19-8 record with the St. Louis Cardinals, posting the best winning percentage in the league. He was 6-3 in 1946 and then 3-6 in 1947. He was traded to Cincinnati in the middle of the 1948 season and finished 0-3. In 1949, he was sidelined after 11 games without a win or a loss. And he was through.

"Bone chips did me in," he said. "I had to give up pitching. I broke in under Billy Southworth. He was managing the Cardinals and he treated me like a son. Then Eddie Dyer took over. He told me I wasn't going to be one of his starters.

"Now, I don't want to make any excuses. But I wasn't trained to be a relief pitcher. To be a relief pitcher, you have to warm up quickly. A starter has plenty of time to warm up, to get himself ready for the ballgame. But a relief pitcher can't. A relief pitcher has to hurry. And I hurt myself trying to be a relief pitcher," said Burkhart.

(*Editor's note:* Southworth managed the Cardinals from 1940 through 1945. His teams in 1942, 1943 and 1944 won 106, 106 and 105 games, respectively, as the Cardinals roared to three straight pennants. In 1945, the year Burkhart broke in and won 19 games, the Cardinals slipped to second place with "only" 95 wins and Southworth moved on. Dyer, who had never managed in the Major Leagues, may not have had as high regard for young Burkhart as Southworth did, but he managed to win the pennant in his first year, 1946, and stayed on with the Cardinals through 1950.)

After the 1949 season, Burkhart's career as a ballplayer was over, but he said he didn't want to give up baseball. He decided to go to an umpire school in Palm Beach, Florida, run by ex–Major League umpire George Barr. He then spent 1952 through 1956 calling minor league games at various levels.

"I was told by Warren Giles, who was National League president at the time, that I would have to umpire five years in the minor leagues or they

Umpire Ken Burkhart is "on his behind" as he signals Cincinnati's Bernie Carbo out in the first game of the 1970 World Series. Catcher is Baltimore's Elrod Hendricks.

wouldn't even look at me. Well, I umpired five years and the next year they called me up.

"I was in the Florida State League which was D ball for one year, then I went to the Big State League, Class B, for a year and then to the Class A Western League for another year.

"Then I spent two years in the Texas League which was Double-A. You can't believe how hot it was in Texas on those summer afternoons. In those days, you always wore a coat. I remember many times after a ballgame I would have to go home at night and wring out my coat. It was that wet.

"You had to love what you were doing because it was hard. All the traveling was by car, from one Texas town to another. If you didn't have a car, you had to make sure your partner had one.

"We got expense money but it wasn't much. You learned to survive on hamburgers and milk," said Burkhart.

"I got the call to the big leagues in 1957, five years after I started in minor league ball—just like Warren Giles had said."

Burkhart said being a former pitcher helped him in his umpiring—but he also took some razzing. "I'd call a ball and the pitchers would yell at me, 'You used to want that one' and I'd shout back, 'Yeah, but I never got it.' Ballplayers love to try to get everything they can get out there," said Burkhart.

"I suppose in the big leagues the games you remember most are the World

Ken Burkhart posed for this photo in 1957—his first year in the National League.

Series games. I was in three World Series," he said.

One was the already-mentioned '70 Series. Another was the 1962 Series. In that one, the Yankees and Giants traded wins all the way to the finish, with the Yankees winning the first game, the Giants the second, the Yankees the third, and so on. The series stretched out over 13 days because of four rainouts— one in New York and three in San Francisco.

Another distinguishing factor was the silencing of some of the biggest guns in baseball: Mickey Mantle hit .120; Roger Maris hit .174; Willie Mays hit .250; Orlando Cepeda hit .158. Burkhart was the home plate umpire in the fifth game, won by the Yankees 5-3 with the big blow being a home run by Yankee rookie Tom Tresh.

Burkhart said he doesn't remember too much about that series. "That was a long time ago. I do remember I was in right field for the seventh game," he said, giving him a good view of the dramatic finish to the series.

The Yankees led 1-0 going into the bottom of the ninth inning. Matty Alou led off the ninth with a bunt single and, two outs later, Willie Mays doubled. Alou stopped at third. With the tying and winning runs in scoring position, Willie McCovey hit a scorching line drive that second baseman Bobby Richardson snared to end the series.

(*Editor's note:* Mays had a part in two other famous episodes in Burkhart's career. On April 30, 1961, Burkhart was on hand in Milwaukee to watch him become the seventh player in baseball history to hit four home runs in one game. Two days earlier—in the same series, Mays didn't get any hits, nor did any of his teammates as Warren Spahn threw a no-hitter.

(Three years later, on May 31, 1964, Burkhart was the third base umpire when the Giants beat the Mets, 8-6, in 23 innings. It was the longest day of baseball ever because the 23-inning game was the second game of a doubleheader. The Giants won the first one, 5-3. The two games combined consumed 10 hours and 23 minutes. Mays was the Giants' center fielder in both games.)

"I'll tell you what I remember about Willie Mays," said Burkhart. "Of course he was a wonderful ballplayer. But what I loved about him was you never found him complaining like some guys do. Yeah, he was a wonderful ballplayer … but he was a wonderful person with it."

Burkhart's other World Series appearance was in 1964. "A funny thing happened in that one," he said. "It's the Yankees and the Cardinals and I'm behind the plate in the third game.

"It's a good game, 1-1, in the bottom of the ninth inning when Mickey Mantle comes up to bat. And he said to me, 'Ken, I'm going to win this game right now' and I said, 'That's all right with me, Mick.'

"Now Barney Schultz had come in to pitch for the Cardinals. He was a tough knuckleball pitcher. Mantle hit his first pitch out of the park and the game was over. Schultz threw one pitch. That was it. Mick said he was going to end it—and he did.

"Working the plate in the World Series is something special. You work hard all the time, but I think in the World Series you work a little harder because you don't want to make a fool of yourself. Like in that '70 Series—I thought they were going to crucify me in Cincinnati."

Burkhart said there are three keys to being a good umpire behind the plate: "You've got to get every pitch right, you've got to get every play at the plate right and you've got to run the ballgame. Don't let the ballplayers run you, 'cause they'll try. Now, Al Barlick, there was a guy who could run a ballgame. Augie Donatelli was another good one. And Frank Pulli is good behind the plate," he said.

Burkhart said he thinks the toughest call is the sweep tag on a play at the plate. "You've got to get position or you don't get the play," he said. The play in the 1970 World Series illustrates his point.

There's an art to calling balls and strikes, too, he said. "As a home-plate umpire, you have to learn not to be too tight with your strike zone. Be consistent. The hitters know what kind of a game you call. That's their job. So you just do your job.

"I used to love Walt Alston. He was a good manager. He used to shout at his players: 'Swing the bat. If it's close enough to call, it's close enough to hit.' He did not like his players arguing over ball and strike calls," said Burkhart.

The more Burkhart reminisced, the more he seemed to enjoy it. "You want stories?" he asked. "I got a thousand of them.

"Now Ed Bailey, the Cincinnati catcher. He was the worst talker I ever saw. He would talk, talk, talk. And he would get himself in trouble with his talk. But that didn't stop him.

"And Fred Hutchinson, the Cincinnati manager, what a nice guy. I loved that guy. But he had trouble with umpires. His problem was: He couldn't talk without cursing. Every time he came out to argue a call, he'd start out by saying, 'You blind SOB.' And, of course, he was in trouble right away. And yet, he'd do it again the next time: 'You blind SOB.' He was a great manager but I'll tell you, he didn't know how to approach an umpire."

Burkhart said Roberto Clemente was a great ballplayer and had a personality to match, but he threw him out of a game once—for using the same type of language that got Hutchinson in trouble.

"It was a bang-bang play at first base and I called Clemente out. And he called me a 'blind son-of-a-beeeech.' And I said, 'You can go, Mr. Clemente.'

"And out came Mr. Murtaugh [Pirates manager Danny Murtaugh] and he said to me, 'Why did you run him?' And I told him what Clemente had said. And Murtaugh said, 'He couldn't have said that. He doesn't speak any English.' And I said, 'Well, you guys taught him some English.'"

Burkhart said cursing is the fastest way for a player, coach or manager to get ejected from a game. But he said one reason umpires don't like ejections is the paperwork it causes.

"You really don't want to run guys, because every time you do, you have to write a report. I ran 15 guys one year. You know what that means? Fifteen reports. Do you know how much paperwork that is?"

He said he remembered when instant replay first became part of baseball television broadcasts, and how people told umpires, "You guys are going to be sorry."

"We weren't," he said with pride, 23 years after he retired. "The replays showed we were right most of the time."

Burkhart said the funniest incident of his career happened in Pittsburgh. Once again, he was behind the plate. He said he looked over into the stands and noticed a woman being carried out on a stretcher and thought she might have been hit with a foul ball.

"What happened to her?" he asked the Pirates' third base coach.

"You called one right and she fainted," he said.

October 10, 1970—When the umpire sat down on the job

BALTIMORE	ab	r	h	rbi	CINCINNATI	ab	r	h	rbi
Buford lf	4	0	1	0	Rose rf	3	0	0	0
Blair cf	4	1	1	0	Tolan cf	4	2	1	0
Powell 1b	3	1	1	1	Perez 3b	3	0	0	0
F. Rob'son rf	4	0	0	0	Bench c	4	0	1	1
B. Rob'son 3b	4	1	1	1	May 1b	4	1	2	2
Hendricks c	4	1	1	1	Carbo lf	2	0	0	0
Johnson 2b	3	0	1	0	Helms 2b	4	0	1	0
Belanger ss	3	0	1	0	W'dward ss	2	0	0	0
Palmer p	4	0	0	0	(a) Cline	1	0	0	0
Richert p	0	0	0	0	Chaney ss	0	0	0	0
Totals	33	4	7	3	(b) Stewart	1	0	0	0
					Nolan p	2	0	0	0

BALTIMORE	ab	r	h	rbi	CINCINNATI	ab	r	h	rbi
					Carroll p	0	0	0	0
					(c) Bravo	1	0	0	0
					Totals	31	3	5	3

(a) Grounded into fielder's choice for Woodward in sixth; (b) Struck out for Chaney in ninth; (c) Struck out for Carroll in ninth.

BALTIMORE	0 0 0	2 1 0	1 0 0—4
CINCINNATI	1 0 2	0 0 0	0 0 0—3

Double play: May, Woodward and May. Left on base: Baltimore 5, Cincinnati 8. Doubles: Tolan, Johnson. Home runs: May, Powell, Hendricks, B. Robinson. Stolen base: Tolan. Sacrifice: Nolan.

	IP	H	R	BB	SO
Palmer (W)	8 ⅔	5	3	5	2
Richert	⅓	0	0	0	0
Nolan (N)	6 ⅔	5	4	1	7
Carroll	2 ⅓	2	0	2	4

Umpires: Burkhart (NL), Flaherty (AL), Venzon (NL), Stewart (AL), Williams (NL), Ashford (AL). Time: 2:24. Attendance: 51,531.

October 10, 1964—Mantle calls it a day

ST. LOUIS	ab	r	h	rbi	NEW YORK	ab	r	h	rbi
Flood cf	5	0	0	0	Linz ss	4	0	0	0
Brock lf	4	0	0	0	Rich'son 2b	4	0	1	0
White 1b	4	0	1	0	Maris cf	4	0	1	0
K. Boyer 3b	4	0	0	0	Mantle rf	3	1	2	1
Groat ss	4	0	1	0	Howard c	2	1	1	0
McCarver c	2	1	1	0	Tresh lf	3	0	0	0
Shannon rf	3	0	1	0	Pepitone 1b	2	0	0	0
Maxvill 2b	3	0	1	0	C. Boyer 3b	3	0	1	1
(a) Warwick	0	0	0	0	Bouton p	3	0	0	0
Buchek 2b	0	0	0	0	**Totals**	28	2	5	2
Simmons p	2	0	1	1					
(b) Skinner	1	0	0	0					
Schultz	0	0	0	0					
Totals	32	1	6	1					

(a) Walked for Maxvill in ninth; (b) Flied out for Simmons in ninth.

ST. LOUIS	0 0 0	0 1 0	0 0 0—1
NEW YORK	0 1 0	0 0 0	0 0 1—2

Doubles: C. Boyer, Groat, Mantle, Maxvill. Home run: Mantle. Sacrifice: Simmons, Shannon. Double play: Maxvill, Groat and White. Left on base: St. Louis 9, New York 5.

	IP	H	R	BB	SO
Simmons	8	4	1	3	2
Schultz (L)	0	1	1	0	0
Bouton (W)	9	6	1	3	2

Umpires: Burkhart (NL), Soar (AL), V. Smith (NL), A. Smith (AL), Secory (NL), McKinley (AL). Time: 2:16. Attendance: 67,101.

Bill Haller

American League: 1961–1982

Rose Bowls Over Fosse in All-Star Game

> "I have one tip for you: Quit swearing at
> the players. You're in the big leagues now."

VANDALIA, Ill.—If you don't catch Bill Haller at home these days, stop by the Moose Lodge in Vandalia. He's likely to be there playing pinochle.

"We play every day—four-handed or three-handed cut-throat. A dollar a game, so when you lose, you don't get hurt; you just get mad," said Haller.

Playing cards with the guys at the Moose Lodge is what he wants to do now. When he was a Major League umpire for 22 years, he was doing what gave him satisfaction for most of his life—even from his preteen years.

"I wanted to be an umpire when I was 12 years old. That's unusual for a kid, isn't it? When I was in the service in 1956, I was stationed in Korea. One day I was over in Tokyo and I met George Barr, the old American League umpire, who was over there doing training schools," said Haller.

"When I got back to the states, I went to his umpiring school. I got assigned to the Florida-Georgia League, Class D ball, in 1958. In 1959, I went to the New York-Pennsylvania League, which was also Class D, and then I went to the Northwest League.

"Everybody has to have a break and I guess mine came when I was working a game in Dodgertown in 1960 and I impressed Charlie Metro, who was managing Denver at the time. [Metro later managed the Chicago Cubs]. After that, I got assigned to the [Pacific] Coast League which was Triple A and got the call to come to the majors in 1961.

"I was in Hawaii when I got a call from Dewey Soriano, my league president. He said my contract's been sold to the American League. I've got to be in Minneapolis in two days. I had to fly to Seattle and then catch another flight to Minneapolis. Soriano told me: 'I have one tip for you. Quit swearing at the players. You're in the big leagues now.' You see, I was a young fart and I thought I knew everything.

"I don't remember anything special about that first game except that it

97

was my first game. But I remember my first crew, a great crew: Ed Hurley, John Flaherty and Bill Stewart."

One of the famous games in Haller's career was the 1970 All-Star game in Cincinnati which ended when the Reds' Pete Rose bowled over Cleveland catcher Ray Fosse to score the winning run.

On July 14, 1970, the American League took a 4-1 lead into the ninth inning but the National League scored three in the bottom of the ninth to send the game into extra innings.

"It was hot," said Haller, who was umpiring at third base. "I drove 260 miles to get to the game and I had a doubleheader in Boston the next day. So, what I want is a short game. And we had it—until they tie the game in the ninth and we get extra innings," he said.

With two out in the bottom of the 12th, Rose singled and stopped at second when the Dodgers' Billy Grabarkewitz followed with a single. Jim Hickman of the Cubs then dropped a base hit in front of A's center fielder Amos Otis, who picked up the ball and fired it to the plate. Rose threw a body block into Fosse, who lay on the ground dazed as the winning run crossed the plate.

"It was a good, clean play by Rose. Pete really belted him but it wasn't dirty," said Haller. "Fosse told me later it ruined his career and it might have. But it was just the way Rose played ... and it was the way Fosse played too.

"Everybody talks about that play, of course, but what I remember most about that game was working with Al Barlick. What an umpire! He was very loud and he swore all the time, but he was a great umpire. He was a 'go get 'em' type of guy. He knew the rules and he could control a ball game," said Haller.

"Bruce Froemming is one of the good umpires today. And did you know he spent about 17 years in the minor leagues? That shouldn't happen. That's one of the problems with baseball and umpiring today. What they should do is have a retirement age with an option to keep the guy who can still do the job. Enforce the retirement age and bring up the good Triple A umpires. That would help the game. That's what they need to do," he said.

Haller worked in four World Series clashes: the Tigers against the Cardinals in 1968; Cincinnati and Oakland in 1972; the Dodgers and Yankees in 1978; and the Brewers and Cardinals in 1982.

"None stand out," said Haller. "It's all just doing a job. The World Series is a little different, though, because it's like the Academy Awards. It's the tops," he said.

Haller later said something did stand out about the 1968 series.

"What pops out in my mind is the fifth game. The Cardinals are up three games to one. Mickey Lolich comes up in the seventh inning. [Tiger manager] Mayo Smith should have pinch hit for him but for some reason he doesn't," said Haller.

The Cardinals were winning 3-2 with one out in the seventh inning—

just eight outs away from eliminating the Tigers—when Smith made the decision to allow Lolich to hit for himself.

"Lolich comes up and gets a bad-hop base hit past second base and that starts a rally and Detroit turns around and wins the game," he said.

Indeed, after Lolich singled, Dick McAuliffe singled and Mickey Stanley walked to load the bases. Both Al Kaline and Norm Cash singled ... and before the inning was over, Detroit had scored three runs on their way to a 5-3 victory. They won the next two games to become the World Series champions.

(What made Lolich's hit—and the decision to allow him to hit remarkable—was his well-known futility as a hitter. In a 16-year career, Lolich came to bat 821 times and had only 90 hits for a lifetime batting average of .110. In six seasons, he hit under .100 and the highest he ever hit was .197. Another oddity: In game two of that same World Series, Lolich hit a home run—the only homer of his career.)

Haller was no stranger to witnessing baseball oddities. A year earlier, he was on the field for one of the most spectacular debuts in baseball history by both a pitcher and a catcher.

On April 14, 1967, Red Sox pitcher Bill Rohr and catcher Russ Gibson both made their major league debuts at Yankee Stadium.

Haller was at second base as Rohr mowed down the Yankees, one by one, inning by inning. With two out in the ninth inning, the young left-hander in his first big league game had a no-hitter going when Elston Howard stepped up to the plate.

"Yaz [Carl Yastrzemski] made a diving catch in that game that was just out of sight. Unbelievable. Without that catch, there's no no-hitter," said Haller.

The count went to two-and-two when Howard took a pitch that fooled him. Both Rohr and Gibson claim the Yankee catcher started to turn, as if to make the long trek back to the dugout. But home plate umpire Jim Honochick called it ball three.

"He only missed one pitch all night, but he missed that one," said Gibson, recalling the game 27 years later.

Haller recalls the next pitch. "It was like it dropped off a table, like a spitter. Howard hit a pitch he never should have hit. And he hit a dying quail just over the second baseman's head. And that was that."

Rohr retired the next batter, Charlie Smith, and settled for a one-hitter and a 3-0 victory. "That was about the only good game Rohr ever pitched," said Haller.

(Rohr beat the Yankees the following week in Fenway Park and didn't win another game all year. The next year, he won one game for the Cleveland Indians and never appeared in the Major Leagues again.)

"The best catch I ever saw was by a guy named Al Luplow who played for Cleveland," said Haller. "He was a short guy but he was fast."

"They're playing in Boston and the batter—I don't remember who it was—hits a line drive and Luplow runs back and dives and lands on top of the bullpen fence and then falls into the bullpen.

"Of course when he comes back up he's going to come up with the ball. But did he catch it or not? I'm the second base umpire and I've got to make the call. And how can I? Do you know what you do in a case like that? You look at the players who saw the play. And I'm looking at the Boston players and it's like they're fainting. They can't believe it. You could tell by looking at 'em that he caught the ball," said Haller.

"Catfish Hunter was the best pitcher I ever saw. The absolute best. A master. I was at third base the night he threw a perfect game.

"I never had a no-hitter behind the plate. The closest I came was Blue Moon Odom one night for the A's. He had one for 8⅔ innings and Paul Blair hit a dying quail—just like the one Howard hit off Rohr—and that ended it."

Haller's brother, Tom, was a Major League catcher who played 11 years in the National League for the San Francisco Giants and Los Angeles Dodgers before ending his career with the Detroit Tigers.

Bill Haller said he didn't have time to pay a whole lot of attention to how his brother was doing. "He had his career and I had mine. Actually, did you know he was a better football player than a baseball player?" he asked. (Tom Haller quarterbacked for the University of Illinois before turning his attention to pro baseball.)

Bill Haller thinks one of his brother's teammates at San Francisco deserves Hall of Fame consideration. "The way they're picking 'em today, Billy Pierce ought to be in," he said. "He had some really good years with some pretty bad teams with the White Sox in the 1950s and the Giants won the pennant the first year he came over to them."

(Pierce won 211 games in his career—most of them with the White Sox—and was 16-6 with the 1962 Giant team that won the National League pennant.)

Haller stayed in baseball for a short time after he retired as an umpire. "I scouted for a while but I was a terrible scout. I'd sit around and listen to the other scouts talk. They'd always be talking about a guy's speed. And I'd always say, 'Yeah, but can he hit?' And you know another thing about scouts? Most of 'em never played."

Every day is still "game day" for Haller, and he still calls 'em as he sees 'em—only now it's at the pinochle table at the Moose Lodge.

July 14, 1970—The game that ended in a "Rose dive"

AMERICAN LG.	ab	r	h	rbi	NATIONAL LG.	ab	r	h	rbi
Aparicio ss	6	0	0	0	Mays cf	3	0	0	0
Yastr'ski cf-1b	6	1	4	1	G. Perry p	0	0	0	0

AMERICAN LG.	ab	r	h	rbi	NATIONAL LG.	ab	r	h	rbi
F. Robinson lf	3	0	0	0	McCovey 1b	2	0	1	1
Horton lf	2	1	2	0	Osteen p	0	0	0	0
Powell 1b	3	0	0	0	Torre ph	1	0	0	0
Otis cf	3	0	0	0	Allen 1b	3	0	0	0
Killebrew 3b	2	0	1	0	Gibson p	1	0	0	0
Harper pr	0	0	0	0	Clemente ph-rf	1	0	0	1
B. Robinson	3	1	2	2	Aaron rf	2	0	0	0
F. Howard lf	2	0	0	0	Rose rf-lf	3	1	1	0
Oliva rf	2	0	1	0	Perez 3b	3	0	0	0
D. Johnson 2b	5	0	1	0	Gr'b'kwitz 3b	3	0	1	0
Wright p	0	0	0	0	Carty lf	1	0	0	0
Freehan c	1	0	0	0	Hickman lf-1b	4	0	1	1
Fosse c	2	1	1	1	Bench c	3	0	0	0
Palmer p	0	0	0	0	Dietz c	2	1	1	1
McDowell p	1	0	0	0	Kessinger ss	2	0	2	0
A. Johnson ph	1	0	0	0	Harrelson ss	3	2	2	0
J. Perry p	0	0	0	0	Beckert 2b	2	0	0	0
Fregosi ph	1	0	0	0	Gaston cf	2	0	0	0
Hunter p	0	0	0	0	Seaver p	0	0	0	0
Peterson p	0	0	0	0	Staub ph	1	0	0	0
Stottlemyre p	0	0	0	0	Merritt p	0	0	0	0
Alomar 2b	1	0	0	0	Menke ph-ss	0	0	0	0
Totals	44	4	12	4	Morgan 2b	2	1	1	0
					Totals	43	5	10	4

```
AMERICAN    000  001  120  000—4
NATIONAL    000  000  103  001—5
```

Double plays: None. Left on base: American 9, National 10. Doubles: Oliva, Yastrzemski. Triples: B. Robinson. Home runs: Dietz. Sacrifice flies: Fosse, Clemente.

	IP	H	R	BB	SO
Palmer	3	1	0	1	3
McDowell	3	1	0	3	3
J. Perry	2	1	1	1	3
Hunter	⅓	3	3	0	0
Peterson	0	1	0	0	0
Stottlemyre	1 ⅔	0	0	0	2
Wright (L)	1 ⅔	3	1	0	0
Seaver	3	1	0	0	4
Merritt	2	1	0	0	1
G. Perry	2	4	2	1	0
Gibson	2	3	2	1	2
Osteen (W)	3	3	0	1	0

Hit by pitch: by J. Perry (Menke). Umpires: Barlick (NL), Rice (AL), Secory (NL), Haller (AL), Dezelan (NL), Goetz (AL). Time: 3:19. Attendance: 51,838.

April 14, 1967—Howard's hit silences the Rohr

BOSTON	ab	r	h	rbi	NEW YORK	ab	r	h	rbi
R. Smith 2b	5	1	1	1	Clarke 2b	3	0	0	0
Foy 3b	3	1	1	2	Robinson rf	3	0	0	0
Yastrzemski lf	4	0	2	0	Tresh lf	3	0	0	0
Conigliaro rf	3	0	0	0	Pepitone cf	3	0	0	0
Scott 1b	4	0	0	0	Howard c	4	0	1	0
Thomas cf	4	0	0	0	C. Smith 3b	4	0	0	0
Petrocelli ss	3	0	1	0	Barker 1b	2	0	0	0
Gibson c	4	1	2	0	Kennedy ss	2	0	0	0
Rohr p	2	0	0	0	Mantle ph	1	0	0	0
Totals	33	3	8	3	Amaro ss	0	0	0	0
					Ford p	2	0	0	0
					Clinton ph	1	0	0	0
					Tillotson p	0	0	0	0
					Totals	28	0	1	0

```
BOSTON      1 0 0   0 0 0   0 2 0—3
NEW YORK    0 0 0   0 0 0   0 0 0—0
```

Errors: Rohr. Double plays: Boston 1, New York 1. Left on base: Boston 7, New York 6. Home runs: R. Smith, Foy. Sacrifice: Rohr.

	IP	H	R	BB	SO
Rohr (W)	9	1	9	5	2
Ford (L)	8	7	3	1	5
Tillotson	1	1	0	2	1

Umpires: Honochick, Chylak, Haller and Drummond. Time: 2:11. Attendance: 14,375.

Ed Runge
American League: 1954–1970

Don Larsen's Perfect Game in World Series

"In a game like that, you just hope to hell that from the seventh inning on, you don't have any close calls."

SAN DIEGO, Cal.—Gary Peters, the left-hander who won 124 games for the White Sox and Red Sox in the 1960s and '70s, had a confrontation with umpire Ed Runge early in his career.

He said he threw a pitch that he thought caught the corner and when Runge called it a ball, Peters took a couple of steps toward the plate.

Runge, he said, bolted from behind the plate, ripped his mask off, and scolded the young pitcher. He told Peters that when he'd been around a while, he'd know that if a pitch was in the strike zone, Runge would call it a strike. In the meantime, don't show up the ump.

Peters lasted 14 years in the majors and said he learned to respect Runge as a "pitcher's ump"—someone who would make the right call when the pitch was "on the black."

In that one episode with Peters, Runge displayed what former National League umpire Ken Burkhart has described as essential characteristics of a home plate umpire—calling them right and maintaining control of the ball game.

Runge knew the strike zone, and players knew how far they could go with him—or he reminded them. He kept a tight rein on the games he umpired for 17 years in the American League, and he was involved in some dandies.

He was behind the plate when Dave Morehead of the Red Sox tossed a no-hitter on September 16, 1965, outdueling Luis Tiant of the Cleveland Indians, 2–0. "Nothing close to a hit in that one," said Runge. "No close calls."

And he was behind the plate on May 9, 1961, when Jim Gentile of the Baltimore Orioles hit grand-slam home runs in his first two at-bats against the Minnesota Twins.

But his most memorable game took place on October 8, 1956, when

103

Runge took his position down the right field line ... and watched baseball history being made.

It was the fifth game of the World Series between the New York Yankees and the Brooklyn Dodgers. The series was knotted at two games apiece and when it was over, would be remembered for a number of remarkable feats:

• It was the first World Series to feature two grand-slam home runs—by the Yankees' Bill Skowron and Yogi Berra.

• The Yankees won one game on the strength of a three-run homer by a 40-year-old reserve outfielder, Enos Slaughter.

• The Dodgers hung in the series with the help of a shutout thrown by Clem Labine, best known as a relief pitcher, while ace righthander Don Newcombe, a 27-game winner during the regular season, was hammered for 11 runs on 11 hits in 4⅔ innings in his two starts.

• Yankee pitchers tossed five consecutive complete games after losing the first two games of the series.

In the second game, the Dodgers rallied from a 6-0 deficit to beat the Yankees, 13-8. Yankee starter Don Larsen lasted 1⅓ innings, giving up four runs on just one hit and walking four.

Despite his awful showing, manager Casey Stengel handed Larsen the ball for game five. And, with umpire Runge watching from his post in right field, Larsen threw a perfect game.

"You're just hopin' you don't get one of those close one-hoppers or trapped balls that could go either way," said Runge, now 80 years old. "Actually, there was a trapped ball in that game, but it was the other way around: A Yankee hit it, so it didn't matter in the no-hitter," he said.

"Back in those days, they didn't have wire screens for foul poles. I remember early in the game, Sandy Amoros hit one down the line and into the seats that was just foul by an inch or two. Back before you had those wire screens, those balls were sometimes hard to call.

"In a game like that, you just hope to hell from the seventh inning on that you don't have any close calls," said Runge.

He didn't. Larsen, who had been so wild in game two, mowed down the Yankees on just 97 pitches, and came within one pitch of walking only one batter, Pee Wee Reese in the first inning.

Mantle made a great running catch on a long fly to left center field hit by Gil Hodges in the fifth inning—the only ball even close to a hit, and the only questionable call by an umpire didn't involve Runge, but home plate umpire Babe Pinelli on the last pitch of the game, a called third strike to pinch hitter Dale Mitchell. Reflecting on it later, Mitchell said, "It was a ball, but what the hell."

Runge umpired in the World Series two other times, in 1961 when the Yankees beat the Cincinnati Reds and in 1967 when the St. Louis Cardinals beat the Red Sox.

"In the '61 series, I was behind the plate in both game one and game five," said Runge. "It was a short one. It only went five games.

"For umpires, sure it's fun to be there at the World Series, but once you get goin', after the first two or three pitches, it's just another ballgame," he said.

Runge got his start when he was umpiring sandlot ball in the mid–1940s. "Some guy from the Big-State League saw me and liked me. We talked and he signed me to a contract. I worked six weeks my first season and they had a one-game playoff at the end of the season.

"Six of us were picked to work that game, one at each base and one in each dugout. The president of the league talked to us beforehand and said we could pick where we wanted to be. The first two guys took the dugouts. I took home plate.

"So with a total of six weeks' experience in professional baseball, I worked home plate in the playoff game. And do

Ed Runge watched Don Larsen's perfect game in the World Series from his post down the right field line.

you know that the next year, both teams in the playoff asked that I be the home plate umpire.

"I worked in the [Pacific] Coast League from 1949 to 1953. My break came when they asked me to work in Cuba at the end of the 1953 season. Now that was really something—154 games in Cuba after I had already worked a full season. But lots of guys watch you work. And four of us got a call that we were invited to spring training with the big league clubs.

"So we went to Florida for spring training. I worked Yankee games. And at the end of spring training, two of us got picked to move up to the big leagues. And I was one of them," said Runge.

"My first game was in Philadelphia. It was a night game. I don't remember too much about the game. I don't even remember who the A's were playing. I do remember that after the game, we took the train to Washington and got there at 2 A.M.

"There were no cabs there. So we had to walk two blocks to the hotel, carrying two bags, at two o'clock in the morning. I looked at Bill Summers, who was a great old umpire, and said, 'So this is the big leagues, huh?'

"I saw a lot of great players in my day. Ted Williams, Mickey Mantle, Al Kaline, Brooks Robinson. Whitey Ford was the best pitcher I ever saw. What made him so great is that he had control ... and he had guts. Those two things make a great pitcher," he said.

Runge's son, Paul, has been a National League umpire for 23 years and his grandson is now umpiring in the Northwest League.

"I didn't pressure Paul or try to influence him at all," said Runge. "In fact, it took him nine years in the minor leagues before he got the call to the big leagues. Some people think that him having a father in the majors may have slowed him down, because to bring him up faster might have made people think he made it because of me."

There's no question in Runge's mind as to the toughest call an umpire has to make.

"Oh, it's the steal of home," he said. "Definitely, that's the toughest call because even though the runner's coming in on you, you can't forget the pitch. So you can't take your mask off and you've got the pitch coming in and you've got the catcher and the batter and the runner and you've got to watch everything. It isn't easy."

On April 11, 1996, 42 years after that night at Shibe Park in Philadelphia when he stepped on a Major League playing field for the first time, Runge took part in a special honor.

It was opening day for the San Diego Padres and they beat Atlanta and Greg Maddux, 2-1. But in pre–game festivities, Runge was asked to take the microphone and get the season started with a phrase that is close to his heart:

"Play ball," he said with enthusiasm.

October 8, 1956—A "perfect" afternoon for baseball

BROOKLYN	ab	r	h	rbi	NEW YORK	ab	r	h	rbi
Gilliam 2b	3	0	0	0	Bauer rf	4	0	1	1
Reese ss	3	0	0	0	Collins 1b	4	0	1	0
Snider cf	3	0	0	0	Mantle cf	3	1	1	1
Robinson 3b	3	0	0	0	Berra c	3	0	0	0
Hodges 1b	3	0	0	0	Slaughter lf	2	0	0	0
Amoros lf	3	0	0	0	Martin 2b	3	0	1	0
Furillo rf	3	0	0	0	McDougald ss	2	0	0	0
Campanella c	3	0	0	0	Carey 3b	3	1	1	0
Maglie p	2	0	0	0	Larsen p	2	0	0	0
(a) Mitchell	1	0	0	0	**Totals**	26	2	5	2
Totals	27	0	0	0					

(a) Struck out for Maglie in ninth.

```
BROOKLYN    0 0 0   0 0 0   0 0 0—0
NEW YORK    0 0 0   1 0 1   0 0 x—2
```

Home run: Mantle. Sacrifice: Larsen. Double plays: Reese and Hodges; Hodges, Campanella and Robinson. Left on base: Brooklyn 0, New York 3.

	IP	H	R	BB	SO
Maglie (L)	8	5	2	2	5
Larsen (W)	9	0	0	0	7

Umpires: Pinelli (NL), Soar (AL), Boggess (NL), Napp (AL), Gorman (NL), Runge (AL). Time: 2:06. Attendance: 64,519.

Hank Morgenweck
American League, 1972–75

A Nolan Ryan No-Hitter

"I worked Nolan Ryan's fourth no-hitter....
His curveball was better than his fastball. He was
actually using his fastball to set up his curve."

TEANECK, N.J.—Hank Morgenweck is the only umpire in Major
League baseball history whose career started and ended with a championship
playoff game.

In between, there were about 10 years of wrestling with what he calls "the
politics" of trying to advance in the minor leagues and then advancing belat-
edly to the majors. He worked behind the plate in two Major League no-hitters and had some colorful confrontations with a Hall of Fame manager and
a Hall of Fame pitcher.

While his rise to the big leagues was slow, his fall from grace was quick,
and, as he says now, 21 years later, heartbreaking.

But, first, how does an umpire wind up in a league championship game
for his Major League debut?

"The umpires were on strike. I got called to work the first playoff game
between Cincinnati and Pittsburgh. The strike ended after one game," said
Morgenweck, 67.

(Umpires from both leagues did not work the first game of the playoffs
on October 3, 1970, and National League umpires, led by veteran Al Barlick,
actually picketed outside of Three Rivers Stadium in Pittsburgh. The strike
ended quickly when owners offered, and umpires accepted, a four-year deal
that increased their pay not only for post-season games but for All-Star games
as well. In the lone game worked by Morgenweck and three other minor league
umpires, Gary Nolan was the winning pitcher as the Reds beat the Pirates 3-
0 and went on to sweep the series.)

He said the regular umpires didn't treat him with hostility that is often
shown toward "scabs."

"I didn't feel like I was infringing. I had spent more time in the minors than most of them," said Morgenweck. "In fact, I had worked with most of those guys in the minor leagues.

"I always loved to umpire. I started when I was a junior in high school— I was thrown into it as a joke, really. I had been working summers with the parks department in my hometown, and one year, when I was applying for summer work, they asked me if I wanted to umpire. They were joking but I said 'OK.'

"I took my lumps. I was a skinny, 16-year-old kid umpiring in a men's league. These were guys who'd just come home from World War II. They were men. I was a kid. So, it wasn't easy—but I liked it," said Morgenweck.

In 1954, he went to Bill McGowan's umpire school in Florida and that same year worked a season of Class D ball in the Georgia State League. He worked the 1955 season in the Class B, Carolina League, moved up to the Sally League (Class A), where he spent the 1956 and '57 seasons, and then spent the next three years in Triple A, one step from the Major Leagues, with the International League.

"I quit after that season. I was starting to see the politics of how you move up, of how you have to know somebody and if you don't know somebody, you're not going to move up. So I quit," he said.

"I umpired college games for a while and didn't think much about getting back into professional baseball. Then in 1969, I got a call from Barney Deary of the Umpire Development Program down in Florida. He asked me to finish out a season, that it would only be three weeks.

"I said, 'If I'm a prospect, that's one thing, but if I'm just filling in, then I don't want to do it.' Well, I did it. So, just like that, I went from working college games to Triple A, the International League. And it was a breeze. I couldn't believe how much the caliber of professional baseball had gone down since I had last been in it. I'm sure it was the result of expansion and so many new teams.

"Then in 1970, Barney Deary called again and asked if I would work the playoff game. And I figured: 'What difference does it make; I might as well.' So I worked that playoff game and afterward, I heard the National League was supposed to be scouting me in '71. Fred Fleig, the National League's scout for umpires, talked to me after the International League playoffs. He said: 'You work with the outside chest protector. We're looking for inside men.' I said I can work either way ... but he didn't get back to me right away," said Morgenweck.

"I worked the plate in the Junior World Series that year and Charlie Berry, the American League umpire, saw me. Charlie was looking for umpires and he told me the American League was going to take an option on me, that I was going to spring training.

"We knew in spring training that four of us were going for one job. Then Jake O'Donnell, who was also refereeing basketball games, quit. (O'Donnell went on to become a great official in the National Basketball Association.)

"So it was down to three of us and, to tell you the truth, I had a great spring. So I got called up to the American League for the '72 season."

Some umpires work their entire careers without seeing a no-hitter. Morgenweck, in the majors for just four years, was behind the plate for two.

"I worked Nolan Ryan's fourth no-hitter. Let me tell you something about Ryan on that night. His curveball was better than his fastball. He was actually using his fastball to set up his curve," said Morgenweck. (Ryan, pitching for California, beat Baltimore 1-0 on June 1, 1975, striking out nine and walking four. Five days later, he took a no-hitter into the sixth inning against the Milwaukee Brewers before it was broken up on a single by 41-year-old Henry Aaron.)

"You know, it's funny," said Morgenweck, "a lot of umpires don't get a no-hitter. The night Ryan threw his, Marty Springstead, who was with us all year, was off because his wife was having a baby."

A year earlier, on July 19, 1974, Dick Bosman of Cleveland tossed a 4–0 no-hitter against the Oakland A's—and Morgenweck called the balls and strikes.

"That was a good ballgame for, if you remember, Oakland had a great team that year," he said. (It was the third straight year the A's won their division crown, the league championship and the World Series.)

"I was from the old school. I didn't want to fraternize with the ballplayers. Things are different now, but in my day, you didn't stay at the same hotels, you didn't eat at the same restaurants, you didn't drink in the same bars. You were friendly, but from a distance.

"On the field, I didn't talk a lot to the players and managers. And there were some colorful ones. Earl Weaver was a character, but he wasn't fun to be around. He had this thing he used to do—he'd pull his cap down real tight on his head and then he'd come out and argue with you. He'd get up real close and jump up and down and beat you with the bill of his cap.

"He did that to my partner one night in a game in Baltimore and got chased. The next night, I'm at first base and there's a close call that doesn't go Earl's way. He came out of that dugout with his cap pulled down and I could see he was going to do the same thing to me so when he got up close and started shouting, I put my foot down on his foot so he couldn't jump. Well, I put my foot down hard, and we wore spikes, so you know it couldn't have felt good. He argued a while and then he kind of limped off the field.

"Two weeks later, we're in New York for a game between the Yankees and the Orioles and I had the plate. And from the first pitch on, Weaver's yelling at me. In about the second inning, I'd had enough. I ran over toward the dugout and got nose-to-nose with him. And old Earl turned his cap around and said, 'You're not going to get me again!'

"He wasn't much fun but he was a great manager, there's no question about that," said Morgenweck.

Morgenweck said he also had some interesting confrontations when Gaylord Perry came to the American League in 1972. Perry won 134 games in 10 seasons with the San Francisco Giants, where he earned a reputation for doctoring the baseball. Prior to the 1972 season, he was traded to the Cleveland Indians for Sam McDowell—and his reputation followed him into the American League.

"I was umpiring the plate for his first game," said Morgenweck. "Before the game [against Texas], I received a phone call in our dressing room from [American League president] Joe Cronin advising me to take a second ball bag out on the field.

"In that bag, I was supposed to put any ball involved in a pitch that looked like it might have been 'doctored' by Gaylord. I was to take each ball and inconspicuously put an 'X' on it with a pen and have the ball boy put it in the second bag.

"Well, by the third inning, I had accumulated approximately 15 to 20 balls that had a brown mark the shape of a nail on them," he said.

"At the end of the game, I was to seal the bag and forward it to the American League office to be examined by an expert for any signs of a foreign substance—so that Gaylord's actions could be nipped in the bud. Needless to say, nothing was ever done about it," said Morgenweck.

That was only the beginning of his experiences with Perry.

"In the 1975 rule book, the new rule was inserted that if an umpire felt that a ball had been 'doctored' and thrown to a batter, he was to call a ball on the pitch unless it went through for a base hit. We were supposed to warn the pitcher. On the next such pitch, the pitcher would be ejected and the league would suspend and fine him," said Morgenweck.

"Well, on opening day in 1975, Cleveland opened in Yankee Stadium and, of course, Gaylord Perry was on the mound for Cleveland. In the first inning, Marty Springstead, the crew chief, was behind the plate, and on one such pitch, Marty called a ball and warned Gaylord. The rest of the game went without further incident.

"However, the following afternoon, prior to the game, a knock came on the umpires' dressing room door. I answered it, and it was Phil Seghi, the Cleveland general manager. It was unusual to see him because he never ever had the courtesy to even say 'hello.' He asked if he could come in and speak to us, which I allowed. He said, 'Yesterday, when you called that pitch on Gaylord and warned him, he wasn't too happy. He said the next time it happened, he was going to sue.'

"Naturally, I lost my cool and asked him if he was threatening us. We didn't put the rule in the book. We were just doing our job in enforcing it. I told him to get out of our dressing room and that I would inform Mr. McPhail [the new league president] about his threats—which I did, immediately from our dressing room phone.

"Cleveland left for Boston immediately after the game and the American League office agreed to let Gaylord demonstrate his 'questionable pitch' prior to game time on the sidelines. The office crew watched him throw several pitches.

"Two days later, we received a letter from the league office addressed to umpires, managers and players," said Morgenweck. "It said, 'Gaylord Perry does not throw a spitter; he throws a sinker. In the future, anyone who questions any of Gaylord's pitches will be severely dealt with by the league office.'

"Those are two occasions I was involved in where there were orders by the league to stop Gaylord's shenanigans, and on both occasions, they didn't have the guts to stand behind them," he said.

"I don't want to give anybody the idea I had a vendetta against Gaylord. I liked Gaylord a lot and thought that his baiting tactics were great for baseball and brought fans into the stands. However, being an umpire from the old school, I felt that if a rule was in the book, it should be enforced," said Morgenweck.

At the end of the 1975 season, Morgenweck was selected to work the American League championship series between the Oakland A's and the Boston Red Sox. The Red Sox swept the series, ending Oakland's domination as three-time World Series champions and setting the stage for one of baseball's most memorable World Series clashes between the Red Sox and the Cincinnati Reds.

It also marked the end of Morgenweck's umpiring career.

"After the playoffs, Dick Butler, the umpire supervisor, told me my contract was not being renewed for the 1976 season. I asked him why and he said, 'We got bad reports on you' and I said, 'Can I see them?' and then he acted like there weren't any.

"That's how they get rid of you. They just tell you you're not coming back. That's what happened to Bill Valentine."

(Valentine, an umpire who had taken part in some attempts to organize American League umpires, was fired during the season in 1968 by American League president Joe Cronin. Valentine said he was told only that he wasn't a good umpire.)

Morgenweck's departure because of "bad reports" on him was particularly puzzling because of his post-season work. Why would someone who was the subject of "bad reports" be selected to work the league championship series?

Was the Gaylord Perry situation a factor? Twenty-one years later, Morgenweck still isn't sure why he was fired. He knows Butler didn't like him too well and probably didn't like the fact that Morgenweck had a fan club.

"I had a national fan club that started in Cleveland," he said. "At the end of one season, I was invited to Cleveland to speak to a group. Butler intervened, and Ron Luciano was sent in my place. I don't know why but I believe the fact

WELCOME
HANK
MORGAN-
WECK
FAN
CLUB

Hank Morgenweck stands below a scoreboard sign in Cleveland welcoming his fan club. Milwaukee second baseman Pedro Garcia is poised for the next play. Note how scoreboard has misspelled Morgenweck's name.

I had a national fan club was one of the reasons the league did not renew my contract after 1975."

Morgenweck said other factors may have played a part. "I hadn't chased anybody that year, and it got to be kind of joke with my crew. I was working with Marty Springstead, Don Denkinger and Russ Goetz and I know in the last month of the season, in the meeting at home plate, one of them was even kidding one of the managers about letting me chase somebody during the game. I don't know. Maybe I didn't chase enough players.

"Another thing that might have hurt me: I had a tough call in Baltimore late in the year. It's the toughest call in baseball. I was the second base umpire and they had us working behind second base in those days instead of up on the grass. You really can't get a good shot at second base from there and on this particular play, I didn't.

"There's a ground ball to third and they want to go third to second to first for the double play. But on the play, the second baseman drops the ball. The question is whether he was in the act of throwing it when he dropped it. I thought he was, but because of where I was, I didn't have the angle. I didn't have a good shot at it. I might have missed it.

"Things like that happened to me late in the year. Maybe that had something to do with what happened to me. And, you know, the next year they changed the way we did things and had the second base umpire move in, where he could get a better view of plays like that. But I was gone.

"You have to have five years to be tenured and I had four. A lot of guys told me I should get a lawyer, but what could I do? They let other guys go, too. Angel Rodriguez, the first Latin ump, was one. He carried a knife and gun around with him all the time, but he couldn't speak English and I think that's why they let him go," said Morgenweck.

He worked for a while assigning umpires for the Eastern College Athletic Conference but he never took the field again professionally. His career was over.

Morgenweck takes pride in a compliment he received years ago from a veteran American League umpire who suggested he might have had a future in a related field.

"One time Charlie Berry asked me: 'How come you never became an NFL official—because you could have been.' It was nice to know he thought I was good enough," said Morgenweck, who had officiated amateur football games years earlier.

(Berry, an American League umpire for 21 years, was also a respected official in the National Football League. He was a head linesman in 12 NFL championship games, including the 1958 "sudden death" victory of the Baltimore Colts over the New York Giants.)

But Morgenweck's heart has always been in baseball. "You know why I can't tell you which one was my greatest game?" he asked. "Because I enjoyed it so much; every game was a great game. And when they asked me to leave the game, it broke my heart."

October 3, 1970—Ump debuts in playoff game

CINCINNATI	ab	r	h	rbi	PITTSBURGH	ab	r	h	rbi
Rose rf	5	1	2	1	Alou cf	3	0	2	0
Tolan cf	5	0	1	0	Cash 2b	5	0	0	0
Perez 3b-1b	4	0	1	0	Clemente rf	5	0	0	0
Bench c	3	1	0	0	Stargell lf	4	0	3	0
May 1b	5	0	1	2	Jeter pr-lf	1	0	0	0
Concep'n ss	0	0	0	0	Oliver 1b	3	0	0	0
Carbo lf	3	0	0	0	Sanguillen c	4	0	1	0
McRae ph	1	0	0	0	Hebner 3b	4	0	2	0
Carroll p	0	0	0	0	Alley ss	3	0	0	0
Helms 2b	4	0	2	0	Ellis p	2	0	0	0
W'ward ss-3b	4	0	0	0	Gibbon p	0	0	0	0
Nolan p	3	0	1	0	**Totals**	34	0	8	0
Cline ph-lf	1	1	1	0					
Totals	38	3	9	3					

```
CINCINNATI    000  000  000  3—3
PITTSBURGH    000  000  000  0—0
```

Double plays: Pittsburgh 1. Left on base: Cincinnati 9, Pittsburgh, 10. Double plays: 1. Doubles: Alou, Perez, Stargell, May. Triple: Cline. Sacrifice: Ellis 2.

	IP	H	R	BB	SO
Nolan (W)	9	8	0	4	6
Carroll	1	0	0	0	2
Ellis (L)	9 $\frac{2}{3}$	9	3	4	1
Gibbon	$\frac{1}{3}$	0	0	0	1

Umpires: Grimsley, Blandford, Morgenweck and Grygiel. Time: 2:23. Attendance: 33,088.

June 1, 1975—Ryan's record-setting fourth no-hitter

BALTIMORE	ab	r	h	rbi	CALIFORNIA	ab	r	h	rbi
Singleton rf	4	0	0	0	Remy 2b	3	0	1	0
Shopay cf	3	0	0	0	Rivers cf	4	1	1	0
Bumbry lf	4	0	0	0	Harper dh	4	0	1	0
Baylor dh	2	0	0	0	Chalk 3b	3	0	2	1
Davis ph-dh	2	0	0	0	Llenas lf	3	0	1	0
Grich 2b	2	0	0	0	Nettles lf	0	0	0	0
May 1b	3	0	0	0	Stanton rf	2	0	1	0
Robinson 3b	3	0	0	0	Bochte 1b	3	0	1	0
Hendricks c	3	0	0	0	Rodriguez c	3	0	1	0
Belanger ss	2	0	0	0	Smith ss	2	0	1	0
Grimsley p	0	0	0	0	Ryan p	0	0	0	0
Garland p	0	0	0	0	**Totals**	27	1	9	1
Totals	28	0	0	0					

BALTIMORE   0 0 0   0 0 0   0 0 0—0
CALIFORNIA   0 0 1   0 0 0   0 0 0—1

Double plays: Baltimore 2. Left on base: Baltimore 5, California 5. Stolen base: Belanger. Sacrifice: Stanton, Remy.

	IP	H	R	BB	SO
Grimsley (L)	3 ⅓	8	1	0	1
Garland	4 ⅔	1	0	1	1
Ryan (W)	9	0	0	4	9

Umpires: Morgenweck, Soar, Denkinger and Barnett. Time: 2:01. Attendance: 18,492.

Art Frantz
American League, 1969–1977

The Carlton Fisk Homer in '75 Series

"He was jumpin' up and down, waving his arms. He
was even blowing. It was like he was doing anything
and everything possible to keep that ball a fair ball."

CHICAGO—At age 75, Art Frantz is still a working stiff. He drives a
truck for a messenger service.

"I have to pay my bills," he said. "My pension from baseball is only $800
a month."

But he's not a bitter man. He talks about his life and his career frankly,
but there's no doubt he's grateful for the opportunity he got. It came late, but
at least it came.

Frantz just missed the big-money era for Major League umpires. He got
his shot in the big leagues in 1969—the year the Major League Umpires Association was being formed. His salary: $9,500 a year.

He was 48 then, believed to be the second-oldest rookie umpire in baseball history. (Emmett Ashford was 52.) Frantz made it to the big leagues without ever having attended umpire school—a rare happening today.

And he witnessed some rare happenings. In fact, Frantz is a part of one
of the most famous scenes in recent baseball history. On October 21, 1975, he
was in Fenway Park and had the best view in the house of Carlton Fisk fran-
tically waving his arms after hitting a game-winning home run in the 12th
inning of the sixth game of the World Series between Boston and Cincinnati.

The Reds led the series, three games to two. Both teams had been idle
for four days—caused by an off-day and three consecutive rainouts because of
extremely stormy New England weather. The game, when it was finally played,
was worth waiting for.

The Reds took a 6-3 lead into the bottom of the eighth, needing just six
more outs to be World Series champions. Then Bernie Carbo, an ex–Red,
slammed a three-run homer to tie the game. From then on, it was scoreless
until Fisk came up in the 12th.

When he swung and hit a towering fly ball down the left-field line, he knew it was gone. The only question was whether it was fair or foul. Frantz, umpiring at first base, tells the rest.

"He was headed toward first, of course, so I was watching him. He was jumpin' up and down, waving his arms. He was even blowing. It was like he was doing anything and everything possible to keep that ball a fair ball," said Frantz. It stayed fair and Fisk circled the bases as the Fenway Park organist played "The Hallelujah Chorus." The Fisk homer also set up the seventh game, which Cincinnati won, 4-3, with Frantz behind the plate.

That World Series was the crowning moment for a man who waited a long time to get there. "I played ten years of pro ball, umpired semi-pro and college ball for nine years and then I spent ten years in the minor leagues," said Frantz.

He displayed remarkable athletic ability before he ever played professional baseball. He was the Chicago city roller-skating champion in 1933 and six years later won a horseshoe pitching championship. In 1944, he was the Chicago ice-skating champion.

In New York, where he got his umpiring start, Frantz played semi-pro football for Rochester and Watertown between 1946 and 1950, and in 1945 he was invited to try out with the Rochester Royals of the National Basketball Association.

But umpiring was what he did best, and for him, it was a labor of love because the rewards were few and the schedule was extremely strenuous.

"When I was in the New York-Penn State League, I laid bricks eight hours a day, then I'd drive three and a half hours so I could umpire a game in Erie, Pennsylvania, and then I drove home after that. It was pretty tough in the old days. I'd get 10 to 12 hours of sleep a week.

"Sometimes my son would help me. He'd go with me and drive, so I could sleep. One thing for sure: I couldn't give up my day job because I was only making $275 a month umpiring," he said.

He spent four years umpiring D ball in that league and then made a huge jump to the Pacific Coast League—Triple A—where he stayed for six years.

"Fred Fleig, the supervisor for National League umpires, told me I was too old. But the American League was expanding and they told me they not only needed more umpires, they needed experienced umpires. And experience is something I had. So I got my shot in 1969.

"I remember my first game was in Baltimore, my first game behind the plate was in Boston and my first 'toss' was Ralph Houk. Now there was quite a guy. He argued with me and he said, 'No bush-league SOB is going to throw me out of the game' and I said, 'Yeah, I'll see you tomorrow, Ralph.'

"He was a terrific guy. You could have a big argument with him one night and he'd forget all about it by the next night. He'd come out and laugh and say, 'We really had one last night, didn't we?'

"He always used to throw his cap on the ground and kick it. One night he took a swipe at it with his foot and he missed it. He just picked it up and walked off. The next night, he came out before the game and said, 'How about that, Art. I missed my hat.' And then he grinned," said Frantz.

"Rod Carew was the best hitter I ever saw and that Baltimore pitching staff that had four 20-game winners was the best pitching I ever saw." (In 1971, the Orioles won the American League pennant behind the pitching of Mike Cuellar, 20-9; Pat Dobson, 20-8; Jim Palmer, 20-9; and Dave McNally, 21-5).

"I guess I'd have to say my favorite ballplayer was Brooks Robinson. It was fun watching him and it's true what they say: He really was a human vacuum cleaner down there at third base.

Art Frantz starred in many sports and got a late start in his umpiring career.

"Baseball's changed a lot because of expansion. There are probably 250 players in the majors today who don't belong there. And it's going to get worse. Look at the hits and walks these pitchers are giving up today compared to their innings pitched. And look at those earned run averages. If you can't hit .300 in the big leagues now, you never can.

"When I played, you faced three or four good starters from every team. I mean, it was tough. And the hitters today complain about anything. A pitch comes inside and they charge the mound. When I was playing, if the guy in front of me hit a home run, I knew I was going down. You didn't dig in. And when I was pitching, I'd knock a guy down, especially if he dug in. Nobody was going to dig in on me.

"The best hitter today is [San Diego's] Tony Gwynn. Now there's a guy who could have played in any era," said Frantz. He also had some special words for another National Leaguer.

"If they keep Pete Rose out of the Hall of Fame, they ought to shut it down," he said.

Frantz remained in the big leagues for just eight years before the mandatory retirement age of 55 caught up with him. "They actually let me stay on one more year, but then I was done. They're a lot more flexible about that today than they used to be."

The Fisk home run game was a career highlight—although every time the 1975 World Series is brought up, Frantz's first reaction is: "I was behind the plate for both the first and seventh games." Frantz, like most of his colleagues, cherishes the memories of his days behind the plate.

(For the record, Boston, behind Luis Tiant, beat Don Gullett and the Reds, 6-0, in game one. The seventh game was another classic, not decided until the Reds pushed across the decisive run in the top of the ninth to win it, 4-3.)

And there were other big moments in Frantz's career:

• Long before George Brett was called out in the infamous pine-tar incident, Frantz made a similar ruling against Thurman Munson of the New York Yankees. On July 19, 1975, Munson had just driven in a run with a base hit when Minnesota manager Frank Quillici protested that Munson's bat had too much pine tar on it. Frantz checked the bat, agreed with Quillici and ruled Munson out.

• Frantz was behind the plate when Jim Bibby threw a no-hitter for the Texas Rangers on July 30, 1973. Bibby, a towering right-hander, was in his first full season in the big leagues and beat eventual league champion Oakland, 6-0.

• He was also calling balls and strikes in Anaheim on September 28, 1974, when Nolan Ryan threw the third no-hitter of his career, beating Minnesota 4-0.

"When Ryan pitched in the 'twilight zone' in Anaheim, he was just unbeatable. He had a great curveball to go along with his fastball. They started a lot of games in Anaheim at twilight time, between 6:30 and 7 o'clock. And it can't get much tougher than to try to hit a 100-mile-an-hour fastball coming at you at dusk," said Frantz.

• The 1972 American League playoffs in which Oakland beat Detroit and then went on to beat Cincinnati for the first of its three straight World Series championships.

• The 1976 American League playoffs in which Chris Chambliss's ninth-inning home run against Kansas City gave the New York Yankees their first pennant in 12 years.

Frantz said he thinks the toughest call for an umpire is the half-swing. "When I first broke in, you were on your own. Now you can get some help. The umpires from the old school didn't need any help and didn't want any help.

"I remember old Hank Soar behind the plate. He used to say, 'If they appeal and I ask for help, whatever I called—that's it.' And he meant it. The appeal didn't mean anything to him and he let us know what he wanted done.

"'Whatever I called—that's it.' Now that's the old school."

October 21, 1975 — Fisk hits dramatic World Series homer

CINCINNATI	ab	r	h	rbi		BOSTON	ab	r	h	rbi
Rose 3b	5	1	2	0		Cooper 1b	5	0	0	0
Griffey rf	5	2	2	2		Drago p	0	0	0	0
Morgan 2b	6	1	1	0		(f) Miller	1	0	0	0
Bench c	6	0	1	1		Wise p	0	0	0	0
Perez 1b	6	0	2	0		Doyle 2b	5	0	1	0
Foster lf	6	0	2	2		Yaz'st'ski lf	6	1	3	0
C.cepc'n ss	6	0	1	0		Fisk c	4	2	2	1
Geronimo cf	6	1	2	1		Lynn cf	4	2	2	3
Nolan p	0	0	0	0		Petrocelli ss	4	1	0	0
(a) Chaney	1	0	0	0		Evans rf	5	0	1	0
Norman p	0	0	0	0		Burleson ss	3	0	0	0
Bill'ham p	0	0	0	0		Tiant p	2	0	0	0
(b) Arbr'ter	0	1	0	0		Moret p	0	0	0	0
Carroll p	0	0	0	0		(d) Carbo	2	1	1	3
(c) Crowley	1	0	1	0		**Totals**	41	7	10	7
Borbon	1	0	0	0						
Eastwick p	0	0	0	0						
McEnany p	0	0	0	0						
(e) Driessen	1	0	0	0						
Darcy p	0	0	0	0						
Totals	50	6	14	6						

(a) Flied out for Nolan in third; (b) Walked for Billingham in fifth; (c) Singled for Carroll in sixth; (d) Homered for Moret in eighth; (e) Flied out for McEnany in tenth; (f) Flied out for Drago in eleventh.

```
CINCINNATI   0 0 0   0 3 0   2 1 0   0 0 0—6
BOSTON       3 0 0   0 0 0   0 3 0   0 0 1—7
```

Doubles: Doyle, Evans, Foster. Triples: Griffey. Home runs: Lynn, Geronimo, Carbo, Fisk. Stolen base: Concepcion. Sacrifice: Tiant. Double plays: Foster and Bench; Evans, Yastrzemski and Burleson. Left on base: Cincinnati 11, Boston 9.

	IP	H	R	BB	SO
Nolan	2	3	3	0	2
Norman	2/3	1	0	2	0
Billingham	1 1/3	1	0	1	1
Carroll	1	1	0	0	0
Borbon	2	1	2	2	1
Eastwick	1	2	1	1	2
McEnany	1	0	0	1	0
Darcy (L)	2	1	1	0	1
Tiant	7	11	6	2	5
Moret	1	0	0	0	0
Drago	3	1	0	0	1
Wise (W)	1	2	0	0	0

Hit by pitch: By Drago (Rose). Umpires: Davidson (NL), Frantz (AL), Colosi (NL), Barnett (AL), Stello (NL), Maloney (AL). Time: 4:01. Attendance: 35,205.

Jerry Neudecker
American League: 1965–1985

His Chest Protector in Hall of Fame

"Billy Martin was a terror from the very beginning.
He wanted you to lie, cheat and steal for him."

MARY ESTHER, Fla.—Jerry Neudecker's chest protector is in the Hall of Fame.

"It's in between the displays on George Brett and Catfish Hunter," he said with laugh. "It's kind of a kick to see it there."

Neudecker, 65, was the last umpire in the majors to wear the old-fashioned "outside" chest protector—a bulky rubber slab worn outside the shirt or jacket.

For about 50 years, one of the distinguishing factors between American and National League umpires was their apparel. American League umpires wore the outside protector, favored by Bill McGowan, longtime umpire and trainer of umpires at his school. National League umpires wore the smaller, more adaptable, inside protector which was the preference of the legendary Bill Klem, who dictated standards for National League umps most of his adult life.

"When I first came up, you were told to wear the outside protector," he said. "Then Cal Hubbard retired as the umpire chief and Dick Butler took over, and in the early 1970s they made it an option.

"The inside protector was used a lot in the minor leagues so most everyone was used to it. It's easier to manipulate. So when the American League made it optional, close to half the guys switched over.

"My style on balls and strikes was the 'over the ear' position so I never had any problem with the outside protector. And you get a lot more protection with it," said Neudecker.

By 1985, Neudecker was the last umpire using it. In his last series of the season—and of his career—he worked behind the plate as the Toronto Blue Jays defeated the New York Yankees to win the American League East championship.

122

New York Yankee manager Billy Martin and Umpire Jerry Neudecker exchange pleasantries as Martin argues a call—not an uncommon sight in the American League.

"A guy came into the locker room after the game and said he wanted my chest protector. And it wound up in the Hall of Fame," said Neudecker.

Just as the end of his career had a mark of distinction, so did his start: He is the only major league umpire to have graduated from Harry "Steamboat" Johnson's Umpire School.

Johnson, a colorful minor league umpire, opened the school in 1950 but died a year later. One of his prize pupils in that lone year was Jerry Neudecker.

"I went from that school to the Georgia-Florida League which was Class D ball," said Neudecker. "I did all of that in 1950. In 1951, I moved to the Evangeline League, which was Class C," he said.

"Back in those days there were a lot more leagues. I think there were 49 minor leagues or something like that. After that I went in the Air Force.

"In 1954 and 1955, while I was still in the Air Force in Valdesta, Georgia, I helped out by umpiring some games in the Georgia-Florida League, where I had started years ago. Then in '56, I went to the Sally League, Class A. Then I went back in the Air Force and stayed in until October of 1960.

"I spent part of 1960 umpiring in the Sally League and stayed there in '61 and '62. They changed the name of it to the Southern League and I umped there from '63 to '65. It was a Double A League then.

"I got called up to the American League at the end of the 1965 season. My first game was in Yankee Stadium. When you go from Double A to Yankee Stadium and 65,000 people, it's quite a thrill," said Neudecker.

"You have to be good and you have to be lucky to make it to the Major Leagues. No question about it," he said. "Sometimes, when you're invited to spring training, there are 10 guys and there are one or two openings. In 1966, there were three openings and there were three of us—me, Marty Springstead and Emmett Ashford. Now that's called being in the right place at the right time."

Neudecker was behind the plate on May 8, 1968, when Jim "Catfish" Hunter of the Oakland A's threw a perfect game against the Minnesota Twins.

"Hunter wasn't overpowering and his ball didn't drop like it fell off a freight train," said Neudecker. "But boy, he could thread the needle. He moved the ball around. Up, down. Inside, outside. He was an absolute master at it.

"The main thing I remember about the perfect game is that in the bottom of the ninth, with two out, he had a two-and-two count on Rich Reese, who was a pinch hitter."

Johnny Roseboro, the star catcher for the Los Angeles Dodgers a few years earlier, led off the bottom of the ninth as a pinch hitter for the Twins and grounded out. Then Bruce Look, a rookie outfielder in his one and only year in the Major Leagues, took a called third strike. That brought Reese to the plate. He worked the count to two-and-two ... and then fouled off four straight pitches as the tension mounted.

"The next pitch was a little inside and I called it a ball," said Neudecker. I could have called it a strike and the game would have been over. He would have had his perfect game. But the reason I called it a ball is because it was a ball."

A's catcher Jim Pagliaroni wasn't so sure. When Reese took the pitch, Pagliaroni raised his fist jubilantly and then shot a disbelieving glance at Neudecker when he saw that it was called a ball. He said later he knew it was borderline, but in a game like that, he thought he'd get the call.

(*Editor's note:* National League umpire Bruce Froemming had a similar experience in the ninth inning of a game in September of 1972 when Chicago Cubs pitcher Milt Pappas was throwing a perfect game against the San Diego Padres. Only in Froemming's case, the close pitch was ball four. Pappas was incensed because he thought the pitch was close enough that it could have gone either way. He got his no-hitter but lost the perfect game on that call.

(He is said to have asked Froemming the next day why he called the pitch a ball. Froemming replied that if he had called it any other way, he would not have been able to sleep at night, to which Pappas replied: "How did you sleep at night after all the other lousy calls you've made?")

In Hunter's masterpiece, Reese swung and missed at a three-and-two high fastball to wrap up the perfect game.

(The sequence of events in the ninth inning, culminating with the Reese strikeout, is recounted in the 1976 biography, *Catfish: The Three-Million Dollar*

Pitcher. In it, Neudecker is referred to as "Larry Neudecker"—symbolic of how insignificant the names of umpires become, even in historic ballgames.)

Neudecker was also behind the plate when Joel Horlen of the Chicago White Sox threw a no-hitter against the Detroit Tigers on September 18, 1967, as the White Sox beat Detroit 4-0 in the first game of a doubleheader. And he was in the field when Sonny Siebert of Cleveland no-hit Washington 2-0 on June 10, 1966. "That was back in the days when the Indians were always in the cellar from the end of May to the end of the season," said Neudecker.

He said he was fortunate in his career to see a lot of top-notch ballplayers, and several came to mind right away.

"Jim Katt was another pitcher who could really move the ball around. He was a good one," said Neudecker. "I saw a lot of guys at the end of their careers: [Whitey] Ford, [Mickey] Mantle, [Harmon] Killebrew. Ford used to carry a hot water bottle with him. We all knew it."

Neudecker was behind the plate when Willie Mays had his final at-bat in the majors. He grounded into a force play as a pinch hitter for the New York Mets in the third game of the 1973 World Series—and was not used again in the seven-game series.

"He had a terrible World Series," said Neudecker. "It's a shame to see a guy go out like that." Mays, second only to Henry Aaron as the all-time National League home run leader, managed two singles in seven at-bats and, in an earlier game, fell down trying to catch a fly ball. To millions of baseball fans across the country watching the game on television, it was a tragic sight to see the 42-year-old Mays, one of the greatest fielding outfielders of all time, sprawled on the ground after missing the catch. Mays redeemed himself later with a clutch hit, but the lasting memory in that game is of him tumbling to the ground. The Mets lost the series to Oakland in seven games.

Neudecker also worked the 1979 World Series—"the 'We Are Family' series with the Pittsburgh Pirates," he said. "That was the series where Baltimore seemed to have it made and then they lost three in a row with three of the greatest pitchers in the league," said Neudecker.

Indeed. Down three games to one, Pittsburgh beat Mike Flanagan by a 7-1 score, Jim Palmer in a 4-0 shutout, and Scott McGregor by a 4-1 score in the clincher. Flanagan was 23-9, McGregor 13-6 and future Hall-of-Famer Palmer 10-6 during the regular season. The Pirates adopted a popular song of the era, "We Are Family," as their theme song with aging slugger Willie Stargell as the "Papa" of the team.

Baltimore provided Neudecker with one of the zaniest managers he ever had to contend with—but his experiences with Earl Weaver began before either one of them was in the American League.

"They say Earl got ejected something like 98 times in the big leagues, but I knew him back in the Southern League both in his last year as a player and his first year as a manager, and I'll tell you something: I ejected him a lot of times down there, too.

"I always had the feeling in the Major Leagues that Earl respected me and I think maybe it was because we had known each other for so long, from those days back in the Southern League.

"I remember one game when Bobby Grich was playing second base for Baltimore and there was a close play at second. Grich sort of stabbed for the guy and missed him and I called him safe. Well, Grich starts arguing and then Earl comes storming out. And before he could hardly say a word, I said, 'Now Earl, don't let him get you into trouble because I didn't miss the call. He missed the tag.

"The next day he comes out, and he said to me he watched the replay of that play on television. And he told me I was absolutely right with the call. Now that tells me something about Earl Weaver. I got along good with him.

"But Billy Martin was a terror from the very beginning. He went out to manage Denver for a while and then was in the big leagues managing in '72 or '73, somewhere in there. And he argued everything. He wanted you to lie, cheat and steal for him. Anything to win. He was really something," said Neudecker.

In addition to the two World Series appearances, Neudecker also worked the league championship series of 1970, 1974, 1977 and 1981.

"Most of the time, a ballgame is a ballgame for an umpire, but there's a lot more riding on it in the league championship and in the World Series, so that makes it a little different," he said.

He worked three All-Star games—in 1966, 1972 and 1976—"all National League ballparks!" he said. One All-Star game in particular stands out.

"In 1966, the game was in St. Louis and it was 106 degrees. They say 350 people passed out in the stands. No kidding," said Neudecker.

It was just the kind of weather where the ideal game would be a quick one. No such luck. The National League won the game 2-1—in 10 innings.

From 1986 to 1991, Neudecker was assistant supervisor of American League umpires, working for former American League umpire Marty Springstead. Now, he spends time each year working with young umpires in the minor leagues.

"The difference between the minor leagues and the big leagues is unbelievable. It's all the difference in the world, not only in pay but in working conditions. Travel and things like that. And yet out of all the guys umpiring in the minor leagues, very few are going to make it to the majors. And if you haven't made it to the majors, you haven't made it," said Neudecker.

"It takes a while to get established in the Major Leagues. You should become more consistent each year. I'd say you need six to eight years in the big leagues before they respect you."

Neudecker said he stays active in retirement by always having something to do—and planning ahead. He retains the classic umpire mentality—decisiveness—and it shows in his approach to everyday life.

"I always have a plan of attack when I get up in the morning," he said. "I know what I'm going to do with my day, whether it's going shopping with my wife or whatever it is. When you get out of bed in the morning, have a plan, even if it's getting up, having a cup of coffee and reading the paper to start your day. You need to have a plan."

And as for that chest protector on display in Cooperstown: "That's the only part of me that will ever get there," he said, laughing once again.

October 16, 1973—Willie Mays' last game

OAKLAND	ab	r	h	rbi	NEW YORK	ab	r	h	rbi
Capaneris ss	6	1	3	1	Garrett 3b	4	1	2	1
Rudi lf	5	0	2	1	Milan 2b	5	1	2	0
Bando 3b	4	1	2	0	Staub rf	6	0	2	0
Jackson rf	5	0	0	0	Jones lf	5	0	0	0
Tenace 1b-c	3	0	1	1	Milner 1b	3	0	1	0
Dv'llo cf-1b	5	0	1	0	Grote c	5	0	0	0
Fosse c	2	0	0	0	Hahn cf	5	0	1	0
(a) Bourouque	2	0	1	0	Harrelson ss	5	0	2	0
(e) Lewis	0	0	0	0	Seaver p	3	0	0	0
Lindblad p	1	0	0	0	(d) Beauch'p	1	0	0	0
Fingers p	0	0	0	0	Sadecki p	0	0	0	0
Green 2b	2	0	0	0	McGraw p	0	0	0	0
(b) Alou	1	0	0	0	(g) Mays	1	0	0	0
Kubiak 2b	1	0	0	0	Parker p	0	0	0	0
Hunter p	2	0	0	0	**Totals**	43	2	10	1
(c) Johnson	1	0	0	0					
Knowles p	0	0	0	0					
(f) Manguel	2	0	0	0					
Totals	42	3	10	3					

(a) Flied out for Fosse in seventh. (b) Grounded out for Green in seventh. (c) Struck out for Hunter in seventh. (d) Flied out for Seaver in eighth. (e) Ran for Bourouque in ninth. (f) Struck out for Knowles in ninth. (g) Grounded into force play for McGraw in tenth.

```
OAKLAND    000  001  010  1—3
NEW YORK   200  000  000  0—2
```

Left on base: Oakland 10, New York 14. Doubles: Rudi, Hahn, Bando, Tenace, Staub. Home run: Garrett. Stolen base: Campaneris. Sacrifices: Bando, Milan.

	IP	H	R	BB	SO
Hunter	6	7	2	3	5
Lindblad	2	3	0	1	0
Fingers	1	0	0	0	0

	IP	H	R	BB	SO
Knowles (W)	2	0	0	1	0
Seaver	8	7	2	1	12
Sadecki	0	1	0	0	0
McGraw	2	1	0	1	1
Parker (L)	1	1	1	1	1

Wild pitch: Hunter. Passed ball: Grote. Umpires: Neudecker (AL), Pryor (NL), Goetz (AL), Wendelstedt (NL), Springstead (AL) and Donatelli (NL). Time: 3:15. Attendance: 54,817.

May 8, 1968—Perfection for Catfish

MINNESOTA	ab	r	h	rbi	OAKLAND	ab	r	h	rbi
Tovar 3b	3	0	0	0	Campaneris ss	4	0	2	0
Carew 2b	3	0	0	0	Jackson rf	4	0	0	0
Killebrew 1b	3	0	0	0	Bando 3b	3	0	1	0
Oliva rf	3	0	0	0	Webster 1b	4	1	2	0
Uhlaender cf	3	0	0	0	Donaldson 2b	3	0	0	0
Allison lf	3	0	0	0	Pagliaroni c	3	0	0	0
Hernandez ss	2	0	0	0	Monday cf	3	2	2	0
Roseboro ph	1	0	0	0	Rudi lf	3	0	0	0
Look c	3	0	0	0	Robinson ph	0	0	0	0
Boswell p	2	0	0	0	Cater ph	0	0	0	1
Perranoski p	0	0	0	0	Hershberger lf	0	0	0	0
Reese ph	1	0	0	0	Hunter p	4	0	3	3
Totals	27	0	0	0	Totals	31	4	10	4

```
MINNESOTA   0 0 0   0 0 0   0 0 0—0
OAKLAND     0 0 0   0 0 0   1 3 x—4
```

Error: Boswell. Double plays: Minnesota 2. Left on base: Minnesota 0, Oakland 9. Doubles: Hunter, Monday. Stolen base: Capaneris.

	IP	H	R	BB	SO
Boswell (L)	7 2/3	9	4	5	6
Perranoski	1/3	1	0	0	0
Hunter (W)	9	0	0	0	11

Hit by pitch: By Boswell (Donaldson). Wild pitch: Boswell 2. Umpires: Neudecker, Haller, Salerno and Napp. Time: 2:28. Attendance: 6,298.

Harry "Steamboat" Johnson

National League, 1914

Ty Cobb Didn't Scare Him

(*Editor's note*: Harry Samuel "Steamboat" Johnson died in 1951. His is the only story in this book not based on an interview by the author. But his story belongs in the history of umpiring. He was to the minor leagues what Satchel Paige, Bill Veeck, and Ron Luciano, each in his own way, were to the Major Leagues. Zany. Colorful. Uninhibited. You either loved 'em or hated 'em. There was no in between. They wouldn't have it any other way—and neither would Steamboat Johnson.)

MEMPHIS, Tenn.—In his autobiography, Harry "Steamboat" Johnson told of umpiring in the Western League when the batter hit a fly ball into left field. It was the ninth inning and the bases were loaded, said Steamboat.

There were some cowboys in the bleachers that day and when the ball sailed into the outfield, they drew their guns and shot it to smithereens, he said.

Steamboat, who had to make the call, provided this insight into his decision-making process:

You don't call ones like that against the home team!

Like Babe Ruth's "called shot" in the 1932 World Series or stories of Ruth hitting home runs after promising sick kids that he would, there is some question as to whether Steamboat's "shooting the baseball" story is true, false or exaggerated. But like Ruth, with Steamboat Johnson, dean of minor league umpires, legend became a part of the man.

His life in umpiring is a fascinating study in contradictions. Consider:

If success is based solely by Major League experience, he falls short. His Major League career consisted of 54 games.

But if success is determined by dedication to a profession, by years of toiling at low pay and little or no fringe benefits for the sheer love of it, then Steamboat is at the head of the class: His minor league career consisted of more than 5,000 games, from 1910 to 1913, and from 1915 to 1946. For 37 straight seasons (1910–1946), he umpired more than 5,700 games. He is said to have never missed a Southern Association game in 27 seasons—4,400 games. He very well may have the record for the most professional baseball games ever umpired. Were he alive today, he would almost certainly claim that record until someone could prove him wrong.

The contradictions continue. Consider further:

Umpires, more often than not, are content with anonymity. Steamboat wrote his autobiography.

Most umpires are satisfied to do their jobs quietly and efficiently with little or no recognition. Steamboat was known throughout the south for his flamboyant style and showmanship. He was a boon to the minor leagues because paying fans would come to games not only to see their favorite teams and players, but to see Steamboat Johnson umpire.

Most umpires go quietly into retirement, hardly being missed. Steamboat was given a "Steamboat Johnson Night" at the ballpark in New Orleans on July 28, 1949.

He got his nickname from an Atlanta sportswriter who thought his resounding voice sounded like the foghorn on a Mississippi River steamer. And his voice was part of his persona on the ballfield. He would call out the names of players loud enough, he said, for the people in the "cheap seats" to hear him.

Behind the plate, he would ride on his heels as the pitch was delivered—stretching up on the high pitches, hunching down on the low ones. There were only two umpires, so each had to be quick on his feet. If Steamboat thought that a play at third base was imminent, he would bolt from behind the plate and sprint to get to the position where he could make the call. Then he would hustle back behind the plate to get ready for the next pitch.

He claimed to have perfect eyesight and he carried with him a doctor's certification that his vision was 20/20. When players or managers questioned one of his calls, he would sometimes reach in his pocket and pull out the card verifying his 20/20 vision and proudly show it to them. Also, on occasion between innings, he would motion for one of the players to approach him at home plate. He would take an eye-cleansing substance out of his pocket and ask the player to put a couple of drops in his eyes. That done, he would signal that his eyes were clear and the game could continue.

He carried a watch in his pocket. Sometimes, when a player was arguing a call, Steamboat would take out his watch and look at it. That was the signal to the player that his time was just about up.

(Other umpires have had similar signals. Legendary National League umpire Bill Klem became famous for drawing a line in the dirt with his foot and telling players and managers, "Don't cross the line.")

In 1939, at the dedication of the Baseball Hall of Fame in Cooperstown, New York, Steamboat was the home plate umpire for a special exhibition game between the "Cartwrights" and the "Doubledays"—featuring players from every minor league—or at least that's the way it was supposed to be.

The game was to be a showcase of minor league talent from all over the country, something that could be repeated year after year as another one of baseball's great traditions.

But minor league commissioners balked at the idea. J. Alvin Gardner, president of the Texas League, wrote a note complaining that to send a player would mean that player's team would lose a week or more of his services (counting travel time to and from Cooperstown) and that would not be fair to the team or the fans.

Most leagues sent players to the game—but not their best players. Of the 38 men who played in the game, only 2—pitchers Johnny Hutchings of the South Eastern League and Joe Callahan of the Three-I League—ever made it to the Major Leagues.

The idea of showcasing the best of the minor leagues in the Hall of Fame game was never done again, so the 1939 game was one of a kind—and so was its home plate umpire.

Accounts of the game said Steamboat kept the crowd amused with his calls from behind the plate—"Strike; a great curve," he said after one pitch. "Foul—I saw it myself from here," he shouted after watching a batted ball hug the foul line.

Another thing about that game that was vintage Steamboat Johnson: Despite the fact the game produced 15 runs, 21 hits, seven walks and five errors, it was over in 1 hour, 59 minutes. Steamboat was a master at moving a game along.

Throughout his career, his chatter was unequaled. He is said to have once told a surgeon, heckling him from the box seats in a Southern Association game: "You bury your mistakes. Mine live forever."

His only shot at the Major Leagues came in 1914. Prior to that season, he wrote a letter to the National League office asking that he be considered for a job. In response, he was notified that he was to be an extra umpire—to be ready to go wherever he might be needed.

In mid-season, umpire Al Orth hurt his knee in Philadelphia and Steamboat was summoned to fill in. He worked the next 54 games, finishing the season, and then was assigned to work the city series between the Browns and the Cardinals in St. Louis after the regular season was over.

He expected to get a contract for the next season but instead got a letter informing him that the league was not hiring him back.

Steamboat asked for, but never received, an explanation from the league as to why he was rejected. Two possible reasons are: (1) The New York Giants, and in particular manager John McGraw, were openly critical of the rookie umpire's work; and (2) his on-the-field antics were too theatric for the Major Leagues.

Whatever the reasons, he never umpired again in the big leagues. In 1915, he began a three-year stint in the New York State League, which brought

him back to Elmira, the town where he spent his boyhood and where his
father had taught him about baseball. (Elmira has another minor league claim
to fame. Fifty years later—and 14 years after Steamboat's death—the city was
the site of the longest scoreless game in professional baseball history: 25
innings, in a game that Elmira eventually won 2-1 in 27 innings over Springfield.)

In 1919, Steamboat signed on with the Southern Association, where he
stayed the rest of his career. He worked some exhibition games for Major
League teams from time to time.

In what was perhaps the most celebrated confrontation of his career,
Steamboat must have been proud that he was able to take on one of baseball's
most notorious antagonists—Ty Cobb.

In 1923, Steamboat was hired by Cobb to work a ten-game exhibition
series between the Detroit Tigers and St. Louis Cardinals that began in
Augusta, Georgia, not far from the home of Cobb, who was the Tigers' player-
manager. The second umpire was from the Major Leagues, Charles "Cy"
Pfirman.

On April 7, 1923, people came from miles around to see not only Cobb,
the hometown boy, but also the Cardinals' great hitter, Rogers Hornsby. The
game was a scoreless tie in the sixth inning when, with two out, Cobb singled
but was out trying to steal. Pfirman, working the bases, made the call. Cobb
argued so vehemently that Pfirman threw him out of the game. But the feisty
old Tiger refused to leave. Instead, he trotted out to the outfield to take his
defensive position.

Pfirman conferred with Steamboat, who was working the plate, and then
Steamboat went out to talk to Cobb. He told him the Tigers would forfeit if
he didn't leave the field. Cobb stayed put, and Steamboat signaled that the
game was over and that the Cardinals had won by forfeit.

Fans, who had paid to see Cobb and Hornsby and the other Major Lea-
guers, stormed the field and were eventually given refunds. The umpires had
to be escorted off the field and to their hotel. Cobb, who fired Steamboat on
the spot, later apologized and asked him to work the rest of the ten-game series
as the teams traveled north. Steamboat agreed to work as far as Memphis,
where he lived.

Given Steamboat's pride and ego—and his hurt in being rejected by the
Major Leagues several years earlier—he doubtless gained a measure of satisfaction in handling the situation, and in doing so, upstaging Pfirman, the
Major League umpire. (Pfirman became a footnote in baseball history 11 years
later when, as the home plate umpire in the 1934 All-Star game, he made the
calls as Carl Hubbell struck out Babe Ruth, Lou Gehrig, Jimmie Foxx, Al Simmons and Joe Cronin in succession.)

Steamboat retired from active umpiring in 1946 and acted as Southern
Association supervisor of umpires through 1949. In 1950, he opened his own

umpiring school in Kissimmee, Florida. Former American League umpire Jerry Neudecker went to the school that only lasted one year.

"One of the things you always heard about Steamboat was that he had written a book while he was still umpiring. He'd get kids to sell the books in the stands before the games. People would get angry at calls and throw the books on the field during the game. Steamboat would pick them up and resell them at the ballpark the next day," said Neudecker.

The book, *Standing the Gaff*, was written by Steamboat in 1935 and subsidized in part by a sporting goods company which had advertisements in it. Steamboat unabashedly also devoted a few pages in his text to praising the company's products.

Former American League umpire Bill Kinnamon never worked with Steamboat but knew of the book caper. "He encouraged fans to throw the book at him if they didn't like his calls," said Kinnamon.

He told another Steamboat story. "Some kid joined the Southern Association and was assigned to work with Steamboat. The kid told Steamboat: 'Mr. Johnson, I'm a plate umpire.' Steamboat said 'OK.'

"About 35 games later, the kid came up to Steamboat and said, 'Mr. Johnson, aren't I ever going to work the bases?' And Steamboat said, 'I thought you said you were a plate umpire.'

"The point was, that if someone wanted to work the plate every game, wearing all that gear in the hot summer and making all those calls, Steamboat wasn't going to stop him," said Kinnamon.

"Steamboat was a real character. He not only worked for the Southern Association, he lived in the Southern Association. It was pretty easy travel for him, compared to other umpires. He loved his work. That's what most people remember him for."

On Opening Day every year, he usually shook hands with the veterans, welcoming them back for another season. After the final out of the last game of the season, he often turned to the fans and shouted "God Bless You."

Harry Samuel Johnson died on February 20, 1951, in Memphis at the age of 66.

Even the medical professionals attending to him at his death had trouble separating fact from fiction: His death certificate lists his middle name as "Steamboat."

Steamboat Johnson's Umpiring Career

1910	Semi-pro, Pittsburgh area; signed first pro contract at end of season.	
1911	Ohio-Pennsylvania League	Class C
1912	Western League	Class A
1913	Three-I League	Class B
1914	National League	Major League
1915–1917	New York State League	Class B

Steamboat Johnson's Umpiring Career (continued)

1918	International League	Class AA
1919–1920	Southern Association	Class A
1921	South-Atlantic (Sally)	Class B
1922–1946	Southern Association	Class A (AA as of 1936)
1947–1949	Supervisor of Umpires, Southern Association	

April 7, 1923—Steamboat takes on Ty Cobb

ST. LOUIS	ab	r	h	rbi	DETROIT	ab	r	h	rbi
Blades lf	3	0	0	0	Blue 1b	3	0	0	0
Flack rf	3	0	1	0	Haney 3b	3	0	1	0
Hornsby 2b	3	0	0	0	Cobb lf	3	0	1	0
Bottomley 1b	1	0	0	0	Veach rf	2	0	0	0
Stock 3b	2	0	0	0	Heilman cf	2	0	1	0
Meyers cf	2	0	2	0	Pratt 2b	2	0	0	0
Freigau ss	2	0	0	0	Rigney ss	2	0	0	0
Clemens c	2	0	0	0	Bassler c	1	0	0	0
Sherdel p	2	0	0	0	Collins p	2	0	1	0
Totals	20	0	3	0	**Totals**	20	0	4	0

```
ST. LOUIS    0 0 0   0 0 0—0
DETROIT      0 0 0   0 0 0—0
```

Left on base: St. Louis 3, Detroit 3. Double plays: Freigau to Hornsby; Bassler to Haney. Double: Heilman. Stolen base: Heilman.

	IP	H	R	BB	SO
Sherdel	6	4	0	1	2
Collins	6	3	0	3	3

Passed balls: Bassler, Clemens. Umpires: Johnson and Pfirman. (Game forfeited to St. Louis because of Cobb's refusal to leave the game after being ejected by Umpire Pfirman. St. Louis wins by forfeit, 9-0.)

July 9, 1939—The "One-of-a-kind Game"

CARTWRIGHTS	ab	r	h	rbi	DOUBLEDAYS	ab	r	h	rbi
Pierro 2b	3	1	1	1	Corona ss	4	1	2	0
Yerkes 2b	0	0	0	0	Collett ss	1	0	0	0
Yeaker cf	1	0	0	0	Belanger 3b	5	1	1	0
Springer cf	1	0	0	0	Jackson c	3	1	1	2
Denoff lf	5	1	1	1	Borsky c	2	0	0	0
Martuscello ss	5	1	1	1	Wilder c	0	0	0	0
Coulter rf	1	1	1	1	Hauser 1b	3	2	2	2
Rand rf	1	0	0	0	Moran 1b	1	0	1	0
Sawyer rf	2	0	0	0	Zimmerman lf	4	0	1	1
Jenkins 3b	3	1	1	0	Strott cf	3	1	1	0

CARTWRIGHTS	ab	r	h	rbi	DOUBLEDAYS	ab	r	h	rbi
Yoter 3b	2	0	0	0	Huffman cf	1	1	1	0
Lowe 1b	2	0	0	1	C. Smith 2b	3	0	1	1
Byrnes 1b	2	0	0	0	Eck 2b	1	1	1	0
Bengough c	1	0	1	1	Nevill rf	2	0	0	0
Schang c	1	0	0	0	Poliomas rf	2	0	0	0
Gabriel c	1	0	0	0	Ruether p	0	0	0	0
R. Smith p	2	0	0	0	Knittel p	1	1	0	0
Callahan p	2	0	1	0	Hutchings p	2	0	1	0
Perry p	0	0	0	0	Webb p	1	0	1	2
Totals	35	6	7	6	**Totals**	39	9	14	8

```
CARTWRIGHTS    6 0 0   0 0 0   0 0 0—6
DOUBLEDAYS     4 3 0   0 0 0   0 2 x—9
```

Errors: Jenkins, Rand, C. Smith, Yoter, Collett. Doubles: Denoff, Strott, Moran.
Home runs: Jackson, Hauser. Stolen bases: Coulter, R. Smith. Sacrifice: Pierro.
Double plays: Martuscello, Pierro and Lowe. Left on base: Cartwrights 10, Doubledays 6.

	IP	H	R	BB	SO
R. Smith (L)	3	7	7	0	2
Callahan	4	4	0	0	3
Perry	1	3	2	0	0
Reuther	0	5	6	1	0
Knittel (W)	3	1	0	4	3
Hutchings	3	0	0	0	6
Webb	3	1	0	2	3

Umpires: Johnson, Moore, Anderson and Carpenter. Time: 1:59
Special notes: Players represented the following minor leagues: Evangeline, Kitty, East Texas, Arkansas-Missouri, Western Association, Eastern Shore, West Texas-New Mexico, Eastern, Pennsylvania State, Cotton States, Georgia-Florida, Mountain State, North Carolina State, American Association, Tar Heel, Northeast Arkansas, Northern, Pony, Colorado Plains, Virginia, Arizona-Texas, CB Colorado, Pioneer, Appalachian, Middle Atlantic, Piedmont, International, Ohio State, Canadian-American, Pacific Coast, Inter-State, Western-International, Southern, South Eastern Three-I, and South Atlantic.

Epilogue

John Rice remembers coming out of a minor league ballpark and checking to see if fans had let the air out of his tires.

John Flaherty recalls being escorted to his vehicle by college football players who were there for his protection.

Ken Burkhart remembers his days in the Texas League when he would go back to his motel room and wring out his coat after an afternoon's work to get it ready for tomorrow.

The good old days.

There have been many changes over the years to improve the lot of the umpire, and two in particular must be singled out:

One. Nothing has changed the professional status of umpiring more in the past 35 years than the evolution of training schools that are run, for the most part, by Major League umpires or former umpires.

Two. Nothing has changed the economic status of Major League umpires more in the last 30 years than the formation of the Major League Umpires Association.

Major League umpires have beaten the odds in making it to the big leagues. But almost all of them point to a break they got somewhere along the way—such as being seen by someone with some clout—to put them on the fast track to the majors. And umpire schools provide not only the training, but the opportunity to be seen by people of influence in professional baseball, giving a young ump a far better chance of advancing than if he had to rely on someone spotting him for the first time on a diamond in Amarillo, Texas, or Kankakee, Illinois.

National League umpire George Barr started the first school in 1935. Four years later, Bill McGowan of the American League started a school.

Back in those days, there were more than 50 minor leagues—and more than 400 umpires working their games. Many probably hoped for a shot at the big leagues some day, where two eight-team leagues required 24 umpires to handle the load. (Three umpires worked major league games until a fourth was added in 1952.)

So the odds were slim for most minor league umpires to climb all the way to the top, especially since most big league umps enjoyed long tenure.

It wasn't until 1946, 11 years after Barr opened his school, that Bill McKinley was promoted to the American League, becoming the first umpire school "graduate" to make it to the majors. McKinley attended both the Barr and

McGowan schools. He was one of about 100 at the Barr school in 1939, and it led him to a $100 a month job in the Ohio State League. In 1940, he attended McGowan's school and got a job in the Carolina league for $125 a month.

Today, umpires don't make it to the Major Leagues without going to umpire school. It's as essential to umpiring as getting a teaching degree is to teaching.

But the odds of making it to the majors still aren't good. About 300 people go to umpiring school every year—and less than one percent make it to the majors, says former American League umpire Terry Cooney, who got his "degree" in 1969.

Another retired American League umpire, Bill Kinnamon, went to the McGowan school, was an instructor in it for a while, and then ran his own schools for about ten years. More than 50 of his graduates made it to the Major Leagues.

Kinnamon says one of the reasons why training schools are so important is because they emphasize things like positioning and timing—the mechanics—doubly important in the minors where the crews consist of two men.

Larry Gerlach, professor, author and umpire historian, points out that umpire schools brought uniformity to the job in terms of students learning how to do it "by the book," and they also added a sense of professionalism where skills were emphasized and individual antics discouraged.

Kinnamon eventually sold his school to Bruce Froemming and Joe Brinkman, both of whom are still active Major League umpires and still run the school. Since 1969, 39 umpires from their school have made it to the Major Leagues.

McGowan died in 1954. His son ran his school for three years before selling it to a young umpire named Al Somers in 1957. Somers ran the school until 1977, when National League umpire Harry Wendelstedt took it over. Wendelstedt still runs it today and Somers remains on his staff. Ninety-nine students from the McGowan-Somers-Wendelstedt schools have made the Major Leagues.

The Wendelstedt school serves as an example of what umpire education is all about. The school lasts five weeks and costs $2,100, not including meal money. Classes meet six days a week, beginning at 8:30 A.M. with 90 minutes of classroom instruction on the rules of baseball followed by instruction on ballfields emphasizing mechanics, proper positioning, and voice control: calling balls and strikes and safe and out calls. The "school day" ends at 3:30 P.M., after which high school and college games are umpired.

While there is no question that training school is essential for umpires to have a chance to advance, the last words in Wendelstedt's promotional guide are cautionary: No one is guaranteed a job in baseball.

Of those who make it through the Froemming-Brinkman or Wendelstedt schools or other similar schools, some are selected to take part in a ten-day evaluation camp run by the Umpire Development Program. From this group, some will be assigned jobs in the minor leagues.

The rewards are great for those who work their way up, thanks in large part to the efforts of the Major League Umpires Association. National League umpires organized in 1963. Six years later, the Major League Umpires Association was formed after American League umpires Bill Valentine and Al Salerno were fired for attempting to organize umps in their league.

The financial rewards umpires have received since organizing are undeniable. Valentine claims that when he tried to organize American League umpires in 1968, he was making $12,000, based on his five years' experience. The umpires with the highest seniority—some with over 20 years in the league—were making just $16,000 a year. Today, veteran umpires make more than 10 times that amount.

The typical pay scale for professional umpires clearly shows the difference between lesser leagues and the big leagues. Wendelstedt gives this scenario:

Class A short leagues: $1,800 a month plus room rent and meal money.

Class A: $2,000 a month plus room rent, expenses and meal money. (Pairs of umpires typically get a motel room in a town centrally located in whatever league they are working. They then travel in the same car from one town to another with mileage reimbursed at about 25 cents a mile.)

Class AA: $2,400 a month plus room rent, expenses and meals.

Class AAA: $2,700 to $3,200 a month plus airfare, meal money and expenses.

Major Leagues: $75,000 to $225,000 per season, plus $35,000 expense money plus first-class airfare; also $17,500 plus expenses for divisional playoffs, $20,000 plus expenses for World Series.

The rewards are great for those who make it all the way to the top—but of the thousands of men who have been called into the profession, there are only several hundred chosen few who have made it to the Major Leagues.

From the standpoint of financial security, former American League umpire Jerry Neudecker is right when he says, "If you haven't made it to the majors, you haven't made it." That's why from the sandlots of Sandusky and Keokuk and Topeka and Spokane to the bright lights of Comiskey Park and Yankee Stadium, it's the love of the game, more than anything else, that motivates the men who make the calls.

Appendix A : Some Umpires Who Also Played the Game

Twenty-eight Major League umpires played in the big leagues before they umpired. Sixteen were pitchers, four were catchers, two were third basemen, one was a first baseman and five were outfielders.

Some had outstanding careers. Jake Beckley played 20 years, amassed nearly 3,000 hits near the turn of the century, and is the only umpire who was elected to the Hall of Fame for his skills as a player. Al Orth won 202 games in 15 seasons and then umpired for 16 seasons. Lon Warneke won 193 games in a 13-year career and once threw consecutive one-hitters for the Chicago Cubs. He umpired in the National League for seven years. Butch Henline was a National League catcher who had a lifetime batting average of .291 in 11 seasons and later umpired for four years.

But, just as is the case with Major League managers, you didn't have to be a great ballplayer to succeed as an umpire.

• Jocko Conlan, a Hall of Fame umpire, played 128 games in two seasons as an outfielder for the White Sox and never hit one out of the park.

• Tom Gorman's major league career as a pitcher lasted five innings with the 1939 New York Giants. His career as a National League umpire lasted 26 years.

• Charlie Moran pitched in three games for the 1903 St. Louis Cardinals and then called it a career … until he returned to the Major Leagues in 1917 and spent the next 23 years as a National League umpire.

• Bill Hart lost 56 games over two seasons in one span of an undistinguished eight-year career as a pitcher, most of it before the turn of the century. Fourteen years after his retirement as a player, he umpired in the National League for two years.

Hank O'Day, George Moriarty, Lip Pike and Chief Zimmer are the only men in baseball history to have been a player, manager and umpire. O'Day pitched for seven years in the 1880s, then managed two clubs to fourth-place finishes in 1912 and 1914. But his greatest success came as a National League umpire, a post he held for 20 years. Moriarty had a lifetime batting average of .251 in 13 seasons and managed the Detroit Tigers to fourth- and sixth-place finishes in 1927 and 1928. Those two years temporarily interrupted an umpiring career that lasted 20 years. Pike and Zimmer had brief managerial stints. Zimmer was a Major League catcher for 19 years.

Conlan's first stint as an umpire came in 1935—when he was least expecting it. He was a reserve outfielder for the White Sox and was on the bench nursing an injury when umpire Red Ormsby became ill in the heat of a St. Louis afternoon and was unable to continue.

Back in those days, only two umpires were assigned to games so there was some question as to how to finish this one. The managers huddled and decided to ask Conlan if he would be a substitute ump for the rest of the game. Jocko said "yes," and a couple of innings later, called his own teammate out on a close play at third. Six years later, he began his 24-year career as one of the National League's most respected umpires and has since been inducted into the Hall of Fame.

Then, there is the situation involving a man bearing one of baseball's great names—Fred "Firpo" Marberry. Marberry was a good American League pitcher who became the game's first outstanding relief pitcher. In 1924, he helped the Washington Senators win the American League pennant, starting 15 games, relieving 15 times—and getting 15 saves. In 1925, he had 55 relief appearances without a start and once again came up with 15 saves. In a 14-year career, he led the league in saves five times and yet also had five years in which he won 15 or more games.

In 1935, he stopped pitching and became an American League umpire. Amazingly, Marberry had a weakness as an umpire he could not overcome: Behind the plate, he called too many balls. This man, who had such a stellar career throwing strikes, had trouble recognizing them from behind the plate. His umpiring career lasted exactly one year. In 1936, he returned to the mound for one more year of pitching in the big leagues.

28 Major League Umpires Who Also Played the Game

Beckley, Jacob Peter
Born Aug. 4, 1867, Hannibal, Mo.
Died Jan. 25, 1918, Kansas City, Mo.
Position: First base; B-left; T-left; 5'10", 200 lbs.

Playing Career:

Year	Team	G	AB	R	H	D	T	HR	RBI	AVE
1888	Pitt	71	283	35	97	15	3	0	27	.343
1889	Pitt	123	522	91	157	24	10	9	97	.301
1890	Pitt	121	516	109	167	38	22	10	120	.324
1891	Pitt	133	554	94	162	20	20	4	73	.292
1892	Pitt	151	614	102	145	21	19	10	96	.236
1893	Pitt	131	542	106	144	32	19	5	106	.303
1894	Pitt	131	533	121	183	36	17	8	120	.343
1895	Pitt	129	530	104	174	30	20	5	110	.328
1896	Pitt-NY-N	105	399	81	110	15	9	8	70	.276
1897	NY-Cin	114	433	84	143	19	12	8	87	.330
1898	Cin	118	459	86	135	20	12	4	72	.294

Year	Team	G	AB	R	H	D	T	HR	RBI	AVE
1899	Cin	134	513	87	171	27	16	3	99	.333
1900	Cin	141	558	98	190	26	10	2	94	.341
1901	Cin	140	580	79	178	39	13	3	79	.307
1902	Cin	129	532	82	176	23	7	5	69	.331
1903	Cin	120	459	85	150	29	10	2	81	.327
1904	StL-N	140	551	72	179	22	9	1	67	.325
1905	StL-N	134	514	48	147	20	10	1	57	.286
1906	StL-N	87	320	29	79	16	6	0	44	.247
1907	StL-N	22	115	6	24	2	0	0	7	.209
20 years		2386	9527	1600	2931	475	244	88	1575	.308

Umpiring Career: National League: 1906

Berry, Charles Francis
Born Oct. 18, 1902, Phillipsburg, N.J.
Died Sept. 6, 1972, Evanston, Ill.
Position: Catcher; B-right; T-right; 6', 185 lbs.

Playing Career:

Year	Team	G	AB	R	H	D	T	HR	RBI	AVE
1925	Phi-A	10	14	1	3	1	0	0	3	.214
1928	Bos-A	80	177	18	46	7	3	1	19	.260
1929	Bos	77	207	19	50	11	4	1	21	.242
1930	Bos	88	256	31	74	9	6	6	35	.289
1931	Bos	111	357	41	101	16	2	6	49	.283
1932	Bos-Chi-A	82	258	33	75	18	6	4	37	.291
1933	Chi-A	86	271	25	69	8	3	2	28	.255
1934	Phi-A	99	269	14	72	10	2	0	34	.268
1935	Phi	62	190	14	48	7	3	3	29	.253
1936	Phi	13	17	0	1	1	0	0	1	.059
1938	Phi	1	2	0	0	0	0	0	0	.000
11yrs.		709	2018	196	539	88	29	23	256	.267

Umpiring Career: American League, 1942-1962

Burkhart, William Kenneth ("Ken")
Born Nov. 18, 1916, Knoxville, Tenn.
Position: Pitcher; B-right; T-right; 6'1", 190 lbs.

Playing Career:

Year	Team	G	IP	H	BB	SO	W-L	ERA
1945	StL-N	42	217 ⅓	206	66	67	19-8	2.90
1946	StL	25	100	111	36	32	6-3	2.88
1947	StL	34	95	108	23	44	3-6	5.21
1948	StL-Cin	36	79	92	30	30	0-3	6.27
1949	Cin	11	28 ⅓	29	10	8	0-0	3.18
5 yrs.		148	519 ⅔	546	165	181	28-20	3.84

Umpiring Career: National League, 1957-1973

Caruthers, Robert
Born Jan. 5, 1864, Memphis, Tenn.
Died Aug. 5, 1911, Peoria, Ill.
Position: Pitcher; B-left; T-right; 5'7", 138 lbs.

Playing Career:

Year	Team	G	IP	H	BB	SO	W-L	ERA
1884	St.L	13	82 ⅔	61	15	58	7-2	2.61
1885	St.L	53	482 ⅓	430	57	190	40-13	2.07
1886	St.L	44	387 ⅓	323	86	166	30-14	2.32
1887	St.L	39	341	337	61	74	29-9	2.30
1888	Brklyn	44	391 ⅔	337	53	140	29-15	2.39
1889	Brklyn	56	445	444	104	118	40-11	3.13
1890	Brklyn	37	300	292	87	64	23-11	3.09
1891	Brklyn	38	297	323	107	69	18-14	3.12
1892	St.L	16	101 ⅓	131	27	21	2-8	5.84
9 years		340	2828 ⅔	2678	597	900	218-97	2.83

Umpiring Career: National League: 1888, 1891, 1893; American League, 1902, 1903

Conlan, John Bertrand ("Jacko")
Born Dec. 6, 1899, Chicago, Ill.
Died April 18, 1989, Scottsdale, Ariz.
Position: Outfield; B-left; T-left; 5'7", 165 lbs.

Playing Career:

Year	Team	G	AB	R	H	D	T	HR	RBI	AVE.
1934	Chi-A	63	225	35	56	11	3	0	16	.249
1935	Chi	65	140	20	40	7	1	0	15	.286
2 yrs.		128	365	55	96	18	4	0	31	.263

Umpiring Career: National League, 1941-1964

Dinneen, William Henry ("Big Bill")
Born April 5, 1876, Syracuse, NY
Died Jan. 13, 1955, Syracuse, NY
Position: Pitcher; B-right; T-right; 6'1", 190 lbs.

Playing Career:

Year	Team	G	IP	H	BB	SO	W-L	ERA
1898	Wash-N	29	218 ⅓	258	88	83	9-16	4.00
1899	Wash-N	37	291	350	106	91	14-18	3.93
1900	Bos-N	40	320 ⅔	304	105	107	20-14	3.02
1901	Bos-N	37	309 ⅓	295	77	141	16-19	2.94
1902	Bos-A	42	371 ⅓	348	99	136	21-21	2.93
1903	Bos-A	37	299	255	66	148	21-13	2.26
1904	Bos-A	37	335 ⅔	283	63	153	23-14	2.20
1905	Bos-A	31	243 ⅔	235	50	97	12-15	3.73
1906	Bos-A	28	218 ⅔	209	52	60	8-19	2.92
1907	Bos-St-A	29	188	195	41	46	7-14	2.92

Year	Team	G	IP	H	BB	SO	W-L	ERA
1908	StL-A	27	167	133	53	39	14-7	2.10
1909	StL-A	17	112	112	29	26	6-7	3.46
12 yrs		391	3074 ⅔	2957	829	1127	171-177	3.01

Umpiring Career: American League, 1909-1937

Eason, Malcolm Wayne
Born Mach 13, 1879, Brookville, Pa.
Died April 16, 1970, Douglas, Ariz.
Position: Pitcher; T-right (only information available)

Playing Career:

Year	Team	G	IP	H	BB	SO	W-L	ERA
1900	Chi-N	1	9	9	3	2	1-0	1.00
1901	Chi-N	27	220 ⅔	246	60	68	8-17	3.59
1902	Chi-Bos-N	29	224 ⅓	258	61	54	10-15	2.61
1903	Det.-A	7	56 ⅓	60	19	21	2-5	3.36
1904	Brklyn-N	27	207	230	73	64	5-21	4.30
1906	Brklyn-N	34	227	212	74	64	10-17	3.25
6 years		125	944 ⅓	1015	289	273	36-75	3.39

Umpiring Career: National League: 1901, 1902, 1910-1915

Emslie, Robert Daniel
Born Jan. 27, 1859, Guelph, Ont., Canada
Position: Pitcher; T-right (only information available)

Playing Career:

Year	Team	G	IP	H	BB	SO	W-L	ERA
1883	Balt	24	201 ⅓	188	41	62	9-13	3.17
1884	Balt	50	455 ⅓	419	88	264	32-17	2.75
1885	Bal-Phi	17	135 ⅔	168	36	36	3-14	4.71
3 years		91	792 ⅓	775	165	362	44-44	3.19

Umpiring Career: National League: 1891-1924

Gorman, Thomas David
Born March 18, 1916, New York City
Died Aug. 11, 1986, Closter N.J.
Position: Pitcher; B-right; T-left; 6'2", 200 lbs.

Playing Career:

Year	Team	G	IP	H	BB	SO	W-L	ERA
1939	NY-N	4	5	7	1	2	0-0	7.20

Umpiring Career: National League, 1951-1976

Hart, William Franklin
Born July 19, 1865, Louisville, Ky.
Died Sept. 19, 1936, Cincinnati, Ohio
Position: Pitcher: B-right; T-right; 6', 160 lbs.

Playing Career:

Year	Team	G	IP	H	BB	SO	W-L	ERA
1886	Phil	22	186	183	66	78	9-13	3.19
1887	Phil	3	26	28	17	4	1-2	4.50
1892	Brklyn	28	195	188	96	65	9-12	3.28
1895	Pitt	36	261⅔	293	135	85	14-17	4.75
1896	StL	42	336	411	141	65	12-29	5.12
1897	StL	39	294⅔	395	148	67	9-27	6.26
1898	Pitt	16	125	141	44	19	5-9	4.82
1901	Cleve	20	157⅔	180	57	48	7-11	3.77
8 years		206	1582	1819	704	431	66-120	4.65

Umpiring Career: National League: 1914-1915

Henline, Walter John ("Butch")
Born Dec. 20, 1894, Fort Wayne, Ind.
Died Oct. 9, 1957, Sarasota, Fla.
Position: Catcher; B-right; T-right; 5'10", 175 lbs

Playing Career:

Year	Team	G	AB	R	H	D	T	HR	RBI	AVE.
1921	NY-Phil-N	34	112	8	34	2	0	0	8	.304
1922	Phil-N	125	430	57	136	20	4	14	64	.316
1923	Phil-N	111	330	45	107	14	3	7	46	.324
1924	Phil-N	115	289	41	82	18	4	5	35	.284
1925	Phil-N	93	263	43	80	12	5	8	48	.304
1926	Phil-N	99	283	32	80	14	1	2	30	.283
1927	Brklyn	67	177	12	47	10	3	1	18	.266
1928	Brklyn	55	132	12	28	3	1	2	8	.212
1929	Brklyn	27	62	5	15	2	0	1	7	.242
1930	Brklyn	3	8	1	1	0	0	0	2	.125
1931	Brklyn	11	15	2	1	1	0	0	2	.067
11 yrs		740	2101	258	611	96	21	40	268	.291

Umpiring Career: National League, 1945-1948

Hildebrand, George Albert
Born Sept. 6, 1878, San Francisco, Cal.
Died May 30, 1960, Woodland Hills, Cal.
Position: Outfield; B-right; T-right; 5'8", 170 lbs.

Playing Career:

Year	Team	G	AB	R	H	D	T	HR	RBI	AVE.
1902	Brklyn	11	41	3	9	1	0	0	5	.220

Umpiring Career: American League, 1912-1934

Kunkel, William Gustave James
Born July 7, 1936, Hoboken, N.J.
Died May 4, 1985, Red Bank, N.J.
Position: Pitcher; B-right; T-right; 6'1", 187 lbs.

Playing Career:

Year	Team	G	IP	H	BB	SO	W-L	ERA
1961	KC-A	58	88 ⅔	103	32	46	3-4	5.18
1962	KC	9	7 ⅔	8	4	6	0-0	3.52
1963	NY-A	22	46 ⅓	42	13	31	3-2	2.72
3 yrs.		89	142 ⅔	153	49	83	6-6	4.29

Umpiring Career: American League, 1968-1984

Magee, Sherwood ("Sherry")
Born Aug. 6, 1884, Clarendon, Pa.
Died March 13, 1929, Philadelphia, Pa.
Position: Outfield; B-right; T-right 5'11", 179 lbs.

Playing Career:

Year	Team	G	AB	R	H	D	T	HR	RBI	AVE.
1904	Phil-N	95	364	51	101	15	12	3	57	.277
1905	Phil	155	603	100	180	24	17	5	98	.299
1906	Phil	154	563	77	159	36	8	6	67	.282
1907	Phil	140	503	75	165	28	12	4	85	.328
1908	Phil	143	508	79	144	30	16	2	57	.283
1909	Phil	143	522	60	141	33	14	2	66	.270
1910	Phil	154	519	110	172	39	17	6	123	.331
1911	Phil	121	445	79	128	32	5	15	94	.288
1912	Phil	132	464	79	142	25	9	6	72	.306
1913	Phil	138	470	92	144	36	6	11	70	.306
1914	Phil	146	544	96	171	39	11	15	103	.314
1915	Bos-N	136	571	72	160	34	12	2	87	.280
1916	Bos	120	419	44	101	17	5	3	54	.241
1917	Bos-Cin	117	383	41	107	16	8	1	52	.279
1918	Cin	115	400	46	119	15	13	2	76	.298
1919	Cin	56	163	11	35	6	1	0	21	.215
16 years		2085	7441	1112	2169	425	186	83	1182	.291

Umpiring Career: National League, 1928

Marberry, Frederick ("Firpo")
Born Nov. 30, 1898, Streetman, Texas
Died June 30, 1976, Mexia, Texas
Position: Pitcher; B-right; T-right; 6'1", 190 lbs.

Playing Career:

Year	Team	G	IP	H	BB	SO	W-L	ERA
1923	Wash	11	44 ⅔	42	17	18	4-0	2.82
1924	Wash	50	195 ⅓	190	70	68	11-12	3.09

Year	Team	G	IP	H	BB	SO	W-L	ERA
1925	Wash	55	93 ⅓	84	45	53	8-6	3.47
1926	Wash	64	138	120	66	43	12-7	3.00
1927	Wash	56	155 ⅓	177	68	74	10-7	4.64
1928	Wash	48	161 ⅓	160	42	76	13-13	3.85
1929	Wash	49	250 ⅓	233	69	121	19-12	3.06
1930	Wash	33	185	190	53	56	15-5	4.09
1931	Wash	45	219	211	63	88	16-4	3.05
1932	Wash	54	197 ⅔	202	72	66	8-4	4.01
1933	Detr	37	238 ⅓	232	61	84	16-11	3.29
1934	Detr	38	155 ⅓	174	48	64	15-5	4.57
1935	Detr	5	19	22	9	7	0-1	4.36
1936	Detr	6	14 ⅓	12	3	4	0-2	3.77
14 yrs.		551	2067 ⅓	2049	686	822	147-89	3.63

Umpiring Career: American League, 1935

Moran, Charles Barthell ("Uncle Charlie")
Born Feb. 22, 1878, Nashville, Tenn.
Died June 13, 1949, Horse Cave, Ky.
Position: Pitcher; B-right; T-right; 5'8", 180 lbs

Playing Career:

Year	Team	G	IP	H	BB	SO	W-L	ERA
1903	StL.-N	3	24	30	19	7	0-1	5.25

Umpiring Career: National League, 1917-1939

Moriarty, George Joseph
Born July 7, 1884, Chicago, Ill.
Died April 8, 1964, Miami, Fla.
Position: 3rd base, 1st base; B-right; T-right; 6', 185 lbs.

Playing Career:

Year	Team	G	AB	R	H	D	T	HR	RBI	AVE.
1903	Chi-N	1	5	1	0	0	0	0	0	.000
1904	Chi-N	4	12	0	0	0	0	0	0	.000
1906	NY-A	65	197	22	46	7	7	0	23	.234
1907	NY-A	126	437	51	121	16	5	0	43	.277
1908	NY-A	101	348	25	82	12	1	0	27	.236
1909	Det	133	473	43	129	20	4	1	39	.273
1910	Det	136	490	53	123	24	3	2	60	.251
1911	Det	130	478	51	116	20	4	1	60	.243
1912	Det	105	375	38	93	23	1	0	54	.248
1913	Det	102	347	29	83	5	2	0	30	.239
1914	Det	130	465	56	118	19	5	1	40	.254
1915	Det	31	38	2	8	1	0	0	0	.211
1916	Chi-A	7	5	1	1	0	0	0	0	.200
13 yrs		1071	3671	372	920	147	32	5	376	.251

Managing Career:

1927	Detroit	82-71	(4th)
1928	Detroit	68-86	(6th)
Totals		150-157	

Umpiring Career: American League, 1917-26; 1929-1940

O'Day, Henry Francis ("Hank")
Born July 8, 1863, Chicago, Ill.
Died July 2, 1935, Chicago, Ill.
Position: Pitcher; B-right; T-right

Playing Career:

Year	Team	G	IP	H	BB	SO	W-L	ERA
1884	Tol.	39	308 ⅔	326	65	154	7-28	3.97
1885	Pitt	12	103	110	16	36	5-7	3.67
1886	Wash-N	6	49	41	17	47	1-2	1.65
1887	Wash	30	254 ⅔	255	109	86	8-20	4.17
1888	Wash	46	403	359	117	186	16-29	3.10
1889	Wash-NY-N	23	186	200	92	51	11-11	4.31
1890	NY	43	329	356	163	94	23-15	4.21
7 yrs		199	1633 ⅓	1647	579	654	71-112	3.79

Managerial Career:

1912	Cin	75-78	(4th)
1914	Chi-N	78-76	(4th)
Totals		153-154	

Umpiring Career: National League, 1895, 1897-1911, 1913, 1915-1927

Orth, Albert Lewis
Born Sept. 5, 1872, Danville, Ind.
Died Oct. 8, 1948, Lynchburg, Va.
Position: Pitcher; B-left; T-right; 6', 200 lbs.

Playing Career:

Year	Team	G	IP	H	BB	SO	W-L	ERA
1895	Phil-N	11	88	103	22	25	9-1	3.89
1896	Phil-N	25	196	244	46	23	15-7	4.41
1897	Phil-N	36	282 ⅓	349	82	64	14-19	4.62
1898	Phil-N	22	250	290	53	52	15-12	3.02
1899	Phil-N	21	144 ⅔	149	19	35	13-3	2.49
1900	Phil-N	33	262	302	60	68	12-13	3.78
1901	Phil-N	35	281 ⅔	250	32	92	20-12	2.27
1902	Wash-A	38	324	367	40	76	19-18	3.97
1903	Wash-A	36	279 ⅔	326	62	88	10-22	4.34
1905	Wash-NY	30	211 ⅔	210	34	70	14-10	3.41
1905	NY-A	40	305 ⅓	273	61	121	18-16	2.86
1906	NY-A	45	338 ⅔	317	66	133	27-17	2.34
1907	NY-A	36	248 ⅔	244	53	78	14-21	2.61
1908	NY-A	21	139 ⅓	134	30	22	2-13	3.42

Year	Team	G	IP	H	BB	SO	W-L	ERA
1909	NY-A	1	6	6	1	1	0-0	12.00
15 yrs.		440	3354 ⅔	3564	661	948	202-184	3.37

Umpiring Career: National League, 1912-1917

Pike, Lipman E. ("Lip")
Born May 25, 1845, New York, NY
Died Oct. 10, 1893, Brooklyn NY
Position: Outfield; B-left; T-left; 5'8", 158 lbs.

Playing Career:

Year	Team	G	AB	R	H	D	T	HR	RBI	AVE.
1876	StL-N	63	282	55	91	19	10	1	50	.323
1877	Cin	58	262	45	78	12	4	4	23	.298
1878	Cin-Pro	36	167	32	52	5	2	0	15	.311
1881	Wor-N	5	18	1	2	0	0	0	0	.111
1882	NY-N	1	4	0	0	0	0	0	0	.000
5 years		163	733	133	223	36	16	5	88	.304

Managerial Career:
1877   Cin   3-11   (6th)
Umpiring Career: National League, 1890

Pinelli, Ralph Arthur ("Babe")
Born Oct. 18, 1895, San Francisco, Cal.
Died Oct. 22, 1984, Daly City, Cal.
Position: 3rd base; B-right; T-right; 5'9", 165 lbs.

Playing Career:

Year	Team	G	AB	R	H	D	T	HR	RBI	AVE.
1918	Chi-A	24	78	7	18	1	1	1	7	.231
1920	Det	102	284	33	65	9	3	0	21	.229
1922	Cin	136	547	77	167	19	7	1	72	.305
1923	Cin	117	423	44	117	14	5	0	51	.277
1924	Cin	144	510	61	156	16	7	0	70	.306
1925	Cin	130	492	68	139	33	6	2	49	.283
1926	Cin	71	207	26	46	7	4	0	24	.222
1927	Cin	30	76	11	15	2	0	1	4	.197
8 yrs.		774	2617	327	723	101	33	5	298	.276

Umpiring Career: National League, 1935-1956

Pipgras, George William
Born Dec. 20, 1899, Ida Grove, Iowa
Died Oct. 19, 1986, Gainesville, Fla.
Position: Pitcher; B-right; T-right 6'1", 185 lbs.

Playing Career:

Year	Team	G	IP	H	BB	SO	W-L	ERA
1923	NY-A	8	33 ⅓	34	25	12	1-3	5.94
1924	NY-A	9	15 ⅓	20	18	4	0-1	9.98
1927	NY-A	29	166 ⅓	148	77	81	10-3	4.11
1928	NY-A	46	300 ⅔	314	103	139	24-13	3.38
1929	NY-A	39	225 ⅓	229	95	125	18-12	4.23
1930	NY-A	44	221	230	70	111	15-15	4.11
1931	NY-A	36	137 ⅔	134	58	59	7-6	3.79
1932	NY-A	32	219	235	87	111	16-9	4.19
1933	NY-Bos-A	26	161 ⅔	172	57	70	11-10	3.90
1934	Bos-A	2	3 ⅓	4	3	0	0-0	8.10
1935	Bos-A	5	5	9	5	2	0-1	14.40
11 yrs.		276	1488 ⅓	1529	598	714	102-73	4.09

Umpiring Career: American League, 1938-1946

Rommel, Edwin Americus
Born Sept. 13, 1897, Baltimore, Md.
Died Aug. 26, 1970, Baltimore, Md.
Position: Pitcher; B-right; T-right 6'2", 197 lbs.

Playing Career:

Year	Team	G	IP	H	BB	SO	W-L	ERA
1920	Phil-A	33	173 ⅔	165	43	43	7-7	2.85
1921	Phil-A	46	285 ⅓	312	87	71	16-23	3.94
1922	Phil-A	51	294	294	63	54	27-13	3.28
1923	Phil-A	56	297 ⅔	306	108	76	18-19	3.27
1924	Phil-A	43	278	302	94	72	18-15	3.95
1925	Phil-A	52	261	285	95	67	21-10	3.69
1926	Phil-A	37	219	225	54	52	11-11	3.08
1927	Phil-A	30	146 ⅔	166	48	33	11-3	4.36
1928	Phil-A	43	173 ⅔	177	26	37	13-5	3.06
1929	Phil-A	32	113 ⅔	135	34	25	12-2	2.85
1930	Phil-A	35	130 ⅓	142	27	35	9-4	4.28
1931	Phil-A	25	118	136	27	18	7-5	2.97
1932	Phil-A	17	65 ⅓	84	18	16	1-2	5.51
13 yrs.		500	2556 ⅓	2729	724	599	171-119	3.54

Umpiring Career: American League, 1938-1959

Secory, Frank Edward
Born Aug. 24, 1912, Mason City, Iowa
Died 1995
Position: Outfield; B-right; T-right 6'1", 200 lbs

Playing Career:

Year	Team	G	AB	R	H	D	T	HR	RBI	AVE
1940	Det	1	1	0	0	0	0	0	0	.000
1942	Cin	2	5	1	0	0	0	0	1	.000
1944	Chi-N	22	56	10	18	1	0	4	17	.321
1945	Chi	35	57	4	9	1	0	0	12	.158
1946	Chi	32	43	6	10	3	0	3	6	.233
5 years		93	162	21	37	5	0	7	36	.228

Umpiring Career: National League, 1952-1970

Smith, Vincent Ambrose ("Vinnie")
Born Dec. 7, 1915, Richmond, Va.
Died Dec. 14, 1979, Virginia Beach, Va.
Position: Catcher; B-right; T-right; 6'1", 176 lbs.

Playing Career:

Year	Team	G	AB	R	H	D	T	HR	RBI	AVE.
1941	Pitt	9	33	3	10	1	0	0	5	.303
1946	Pitt	7	21	2	4	0	0	0	0	.190
2 yrs.		16	54	5	14	1	0	0	5	.259

Umpiring Career: National League, 1957-1965

Swartwood, Cyrus ("Ed")
Born, Jan. 12, 1859, Rockford, Ill.
Died May 10, 1924, Pittsburgh, Pa.
POSITION: Pitcher; B-left; T-right 6', 198 lbs.

Playing Career:

Year	Team	G	IP	H	BB	SO	W-L	ERA
1884	Pitt	1	2 ⅓	6	1	0	0-0	11.57
1885	Tol	1	3	2	0	1	0-0	3.00
2 years		2	5 ⅓	8	1	1	0-0	6.75

Umpiring Career: National League, 1894-1900

Warneke, Lonnie
Born March 28, 1909, Mt. Ida, Ark.
Died June 23, 1976, Hot Springs Ark.
Position: Pitcher; B-right; T-right; 6'2", 185 lbs.

Playing Career:

Year	Team	G	IP	H	BB	SO	W-L	ERA
1930	Chi-N	1	1 ⅓	2	5	0	0-0	33.75
1931	Chi-N	20	64 ⅓	67	37	27	2-4	3.22

Year	Team	G	IP	H	BB	SO	W-L	ERA
1932	Chi-N	35	277	247	64	106	22-6	2.37
1933	Chi-N	36	287 ⅓	262	75	133	18-13	2.00
1934	Chi-N	43	291 ⅓	273	66	143	22-10	3.21
1935	Chi-N	42	261 ⅔	257	50	120	20-13	3.06
1936	Chi-N	40	240 ⅔	246	76	113	16-13	3.44
1937	StL-N	36	238 ⅔	280	69	87	18-11	4.50
1938	StL-N	31	197	199	64	89	13-8	3.97
1939	StL-N	34	262	160	49	59	13-7	3.78
1940	StL-N	33	232	235	47	85	16-10	3.14
1941	StL-N	37	246	227	82	83	17-9	3.15
1942	StL-Chi-N	27	181	173	36	59	11-11	2.73
1943	Chi-N	21	88 ⅓	82	18	30	4-5	3.16
1945	Chi-N	9	14	16	1	6	1-1	2.86
15 yrs.		445	2782 ⅔	2726	739	1140	193-121	3.18

Umpiring Career: National League, 1949-1955

Zimmer, Charles Louis ("Chief")
Born Nov. 23, 1860, Marietta, Ohio
Died Aug. 22, 1949, Cleveland, Ohio
Position: Catcher; B-right; T-right; 6', 190 lbs

Playing Career:

Year	Team	G	AB	R	H	D	T	HR	RBI	AVE
1884	Det	8	29	0	2	1	0	0	0	.069
1886	NY	8	19	1	3	0	0	0	0	.158
1887	Cleve	14	52	9	12	5	0	0	0	.231
1888	Cleve	65	212	27	51	11	4	0	22	.241
1889	Cleve	84	259	47	67	9	9	1	21	.259
1890	Cleve	125	444	54	95	16	6	2	57	.214
1891	Cleve	116	440	55	112	21	4	3	69	.255
1892	Cleve	111	413	63	108	29	13	1	64	.282
1893	Cleve	57	227	27	70	13	7	2	41	.308
1894	Cleve	90	341	55	97	20	5	4	65	.284
1895	Cleve	88	315	60	107	21	2	5	56	.340
1896	Cleve	91	336	46	93	18	3	5	46	.277
1897	Cleve	80	294	50	93	22	3	0	40	.316
1898	Cleve	20	63	5	15	2	0	0	40	.238
1899	Cle-Lou	95	335	52	103	13	4	4	43	.307
1900	Pitt	82	271	27	80	7	10	0	35	.295
1901	Pitt	69	236	17	52	7	3	0	21	.220
1902	Pitt	42	142	13	38	4	2	0	13	.268
1903	Phil-N	37	118	9	26	2	1	1	9	.220
19 years		1280	4546	617	1224	222	76	26	617	.269

Managerial Career:
1903   Phil-N   49-86   (7th)
Umpiring Career: National League, 1889, 1904-1905

Appendix B : A Chronology of Major League Umpiring

1876—Billy McLean umpires first National League game.

1901—Thomas H. Connolly umpires first American League game.

1903—Hank O'Day and Tom Connolly become first World Series umpiring crew.

1905—Cy Rigler, while working in minor leagues, raises his right hand to signify called strikes, a practice that will catch on.

1906—Billy Evans (AL) becomes a Major League umpire at the age of 22—still a record as youngest umpire.

1906—Because of the speed and dexterity of the athletes, the American League begins using two umpires in games instead of one.

1908—Two-man umpiring crews are used for the first time in the World Series.

1909—Baseball begins using four-man crews in the World Series, a practice that would continue for 37 years.

1912—The National League adopts the American League practice of using two umpires.

1917—In possibly the most famous ejection in baseball history, umpire Brick Owens ejects Boston pitcher Babe Ruth after Ruth walked the first batter of the game. Relief pitcher Ernie Shore picked off the baserunner and retired the next 26 batters.

1933—A third umpire is added to Major League crews.

1933—Bill Dineen, Bill Klem, Bill McGowan and Cy Rigler become the first All-Star umpiring crew.

1934—American League umpire George Hildebrand retires, taking with him a record that still stands. He umpired in 3,510 consecutive games, a span of nearly 23 years.

1935—George Barr opens first umpire training school.

1935—When umpire Red Ormsby becomes ill in a game between the Chicago White Sox and St. Louis Browns, both managers agree to use a reserve Chicago player as a substitute. His name is Jocko Conlan. Forty years later, he will be in the Hall of Fame.

1937—Umpires' pay is raised to a minimum of $4,000 and maximum of $10,000.

1939—Bill McGowan opens second umpire training school.

1941—Bill Klem retires after a record 37 years in Major Leagues, a career that included 18 World Series appearances in 108 World Series games, both also records.

1941—Tom Connolly becomes the American League's first umpire in chief.

1942—Umpires' pay is raised to a minimum of $5,000 and a maximum of $12,000.

1945—Ernie Stewart (AL), accused of trying to organize umpires, is fired by American League president Will Harridge.

1946—Bill McKinley (AL) becomes first graduate of umpire training school to make the Major Leagues.

1947—Six-man crews are used for the first time in the World Series.

1949—Umpires have to adjust to a new strike zone—shortened to between the batter's armpits and the top of his knees.

1949—Six-man crews are used for the first time in the All-Star game.

1950—Henry S. "Steamboat" Johnson, a minor league umpire for 40 years, starts an umpire school. It exists for only a year, but one of its graduates, Jerry Neudecker, eventually makes it to the Major Leagues.

1951—Bill Valentine (18) becomes professional baseball's youngest umpire.

1951—Emmett Ashford becomes the first black umpire in professional baseball, signing with the Southwestern International League.

1951—Umpire Ed Hurley asks to see the player's contract, then allows midget Eddie Gaedel to bat in a Major League game.

1952—A fourth umpire is added to Major League crews.

1953—Tom Connolly (AL) and Bill Klem (NL) are elected to the Hall of Fame.

1953—Umpires' pay is raised to a minimum of $6,000 and a maximum of $16,000.

1954—Bill McGowan retires, ending an American League career that included a stretch of 2,541 games without missing an inning.

1956—Babe Pinelli works behind the plate for the last time in his career—Don Larsen's perfect game in the World Series.

1957—Al Somers takes over Bill McGowan's Umpire School which had been run by McGowan's son since McGowan's death in November 1954.

1963—National League Umpires Association formed.

1963—Umpires have to adjust to a new strike zone again; it is changed back to its original form—from the top of the batter's shoulders to the bottom of his knees.

1966—Emmett Ashford (AL) becomes first black umpire in the Major Leagues.

1968—Bill Valentine and Alex Salerno (AL) are fired in mid-season by American League president Joe Cronin after they investigated possibilities of starting an American League umpires association.

1969—After a season in which Bob Gibson finished with a 1.12 earned run average, Dennis McLain won 31 games, Don Drysdale pitched 58 consecutive scoreless innings, Jim "Catfish" Hunter threw a perfect game, and Ray Washburn of St. Louis and Gaylord Perry of San Francisco threw no- hitters on consecutive days when their teams were playing each other, the Major League Rules Committee shortens the strike zone, and umpires have to adjust once again.

1969—Bill Kinnamon, an American League umpire who was forced by an injury to retire in 1969, helps start an instructional program for umpires, subsidized by both the American and National Leagues.

1970—Umpires stage their first strike, which lasts one day, October 3, the day major league playoffs are to begin.

1970—As a result of the strike, the Major League Umpires Association is recognized and a new labor contract assures umpires of a minimum salary of $11,000 and a maximum of $21,000.

1973—Art Williams becomes the first black umpire in the National League.

1973—Billy Evans (AL) is elected to the Hall of Fame.

1974—Armando Rodriguez (AL) becomes the first Latin-American umpire in the Major Leagues.

1974—Jocko Conlan (NL) is elected to the Hall of Fame.

1976—Cal Hubbard (AL) is elected to the Hall of Fame.

1977—Harry Wendelstedt takes over Al Somers' umpiring school and keeps Somers on staff.

1978—A second umpires strike lasts one day and is ended by a court injunction.

1979—A third strike, which lasts from opening day until May 18, results in umpires receiving a minimum salary of $22,000, a maximum of $55,000, no-cut contracts, $77 a day per diem, and two weeks vacation during the season.

1983—Responding to a *New York Times* survey, Major League players rate Steve Palermo as the best umpire in the American League and Dutch Rennert as the best in the National League.

1983—In one of the most famous disputed calls, umpire Tim McClelland takes a home run away from Kansas City's George Brett for using an illegal bat in what came to be known as "the pine tar incident."

1984—Major League umpires, seeking better pay for playoff and World Series games, strike at the start of the playoffs, causing replacement umpires to work several of the games.

1985—Another umpire strike is averted when an arbitrator awards umpires a 40 percent increase to work the expanded, seven-game playoff system. The arbitrator is former president Richard Nixon.

1986—Both leagues adopt the inside chest protector as standard gear. American League umpire Jerry Neudecker's outside protector, the last one used in the majors, goes to the Hall of Fame.

1989—Al Barlick (NL) is elected to the Hall of Fame.

1990—Umpire Terry Cooney ejects Boston pitcher Roger Clemens from a playoff game against Oakland, stirring memories of the ejection of another Boston pitcher 73 years earlier—Babe Ruth.

1991—American League umpire Steve Palermo is shot and seriously wounded in the parking lot of a Dallas restaurant, ending his Major League umpiring career.

1992—Bill McGowan (AL) is elected to the Hall of Fame.

1996—John McSherry (NL), umpiring behind the plate in Cincinnati, collapses on the field and dies of a heart attack on April 1.

Appendix C : A Roster of
Major League Umpires from 1876 On

Prior to 1900 (All National League)

Abbey, Charles 1897
Adams, James 1897
Allen, Hezekiah 1876
Anderson, William 1890
Andrews, G. Edward 1889, 1893, 1895, 1898–99
Arundel, John 1888

Barnie, William S. 1892
Battin, Joseph V. 1891
Betts, William G. 1894–96, 1898–99
Boles, Charles 1877
Bond, Thomas H. 1883, 1885
Bradley, George H. 1879–83
Brady, Jackson 1887
Bredburg, George W. 1877
Brennan, John E. 1899
Brown, Thomas T. 1898–99 (also 1901–02)
Bunce, Joshua 1877
Burnham, George W. 1883, 1889, 1895
Burns, John S. 1884
Burns, Thomas E. 1892
Burns, Thomas P. 1899
Burtis, L.W. 1876–77

Callahan, William J. 1881

Campbell, Daniel 1894–96
Carpenter, William B. 1897 (also 1904, 1906–07)
Chapman, John C. 1880
Chipman, Harry F. 1883, 1885
Conahan (no first name available) 1886
Cone, J. F. 1877
Connolly, John M. 1886
Connolly, Thomas H. 1898–1900
Crandall, Robert 1877
Cross, John A. 1878
Curry, Wesley 1885–86, 1889, 1898
Cushman, Charles H. 1885, 1898

Dailey, John J. 1882
Daniels, Charles F. 1876, 1878–80, 1887–88
Decker, Stewart M. 1883–85, 1888
Devinney, P. H. 1877
Doscher, John H. Sr. 1880–81, 1887
Ducharme (no first name available) 1876–77
Dunnigan, Joseph 1881–82
Dwyer, J. Francis "Frank" 1899 (also 1901)

Eagan, John J. 1878, 1886
Ellick, Joseph J. 1886
Emslie, Robert D. 1891–1924

Ferguson, Robert V. 1879, 1884–85
Fessenden, Wallace C. 1889–90
Fountain, Edward G. 1879
Fulmer, Charles J. 1886
Furlong, William E. 1878–79,
    1883–84

Gaffney John H. 1884–86, 1891–94,
    1899–1900
Galvin James F. 1895
Gillean, Thomas 1879–80
Gunning, Thomas F. 1877

Hautz, Charles A. 1876, 1879
Henderson, J. Harding 1895–96
Hengle, Edward S. 1887
Heuble, George A. 1876
Heydler, John A. 1898
Higham, Richard 1881–82
Hoagland, Willard A. 1894
Hodges, A. D. 1876
Holland, John A. 1877
Hornung, M. Joseph 1893, 1896
Hunt, John T. 1895, 1898–99
Hurst, Timothy C. 1891–97 (also
    1900, 1903)

Jeffers, W. W. 1881
Jevne, Frederick 1895
Julian, Joseph O. 1878

Keefe, Timothy J. 1894–96
Kelly, John O. 1882, 1888, 1897
Kenney, John 1877
Knight, Alonzo P. 1889

Lane, Frank H. 1883
Latham, W. Arlington 1899 (also
    1902)

Long, William H. 1895
Lynch, Thomas J. 1888–99

McDermott, Michael J. 1890, 1897
McDonald, James F. 1895, 1897–99
McElwee, Harvey 1877
McFarland, Horace 1896–97
McGarr, James B. 1899
McLaughlin, Michael 1893
McLean, William H. 1876,
    1878–80, 1882–84
McQuaid, John H. 1889–94
Macullar, James F. 1892
Mahoney, Michael J. 1892
Malone, Ferguson G. 1884
Manassau, Alfred S. 1899
Mathews, Robert T. 1880
Miller, George E. 1879
Mitchell, Charles 1892

O'Day, Henry F. 1895, 1897–1911
    (also 1913, 1915–27)
Odlin, Albert F. 1883

Pearce, Richard J. 1878–82
Pears, Frank 1897 (also 1905)
Pierce, Grayson S. 1886–87
Powers, Philip J. 1879, 1881,
    1886–91
Pratt, Albert G. 1879
Pratt, Thomas J. 1886

Quest, Joseph L. 1886–87
Quinn, Joseph C. 1882

Riley, William J. 1880

Seward, Edward 1893
Seward, George E. 1876, 1878
Sheridan, John F. 1892, 1896–97
Smith, Charles M. 1881
Smith, William W. 1898–89
Snyder, Charles N. "Pop" 1892–93, 1898–1901
Stage, Charles W. 1894
Stambaugh, Calvin G. 1877–78
Strief, George A. 1890
Sullivan, David F. 1882, 1885
Sullivan, Jeremiah, 1887
Sullivan, T. P. 1880
Summer, James G. 1877
Swartwood, C. Edward 1894, 1898–1900

Tilden, Otis 1880

Valentine, John G. 1887–88
Van Court, Eugene 1884

Walker, William E. 1876–77
Walsh, Michael F. 1876, 1878, 1880
Warner, Albert 1898–1900
Weidman, George E. "Stump" 1896
White, Gideon F. 1878
Wilbur, Charles E. 1879
Wilson, John A. 1887
Wise, Samuel W. 1889, 1893
Wood, George A. 1898

York, Thomas J. 1886
Young, Joseph 1879

Zacharias, Thomas 1890

1900 to present: National League

Baker, William P. 1957
Ballanfant, E. Lee 1936–57; died July 15, 1987
Barlick, Albert J. 1940–43, 1946–55, 1958–71; elected to Hall of Fame 1989; died 1995
Barnes, Ronald 1990–present
Barr, George M. 1932–49; died July 26, 1974
Barron, Mark E. 1992–present
Bausewine, George 1905
Behle, Frank 1901
Bell, Wally 1992–present
Betz, Edwin G. 1961
Boggess, Lynton R. "Dusty" 1944–48, 1950–62; died July 8, 1968
Bonin, Gregory 1986–present
Bransfield, William E. 1917; died May 1, 1947
Brennan, William T. 1909–13, 1921
Brocklander, Fred W. 1979–90
Brown, Thomas T. 1898–99, 1901–1902
Burkhart, W. Kenneth 1957–73
Bush, Garnet C. 1911–1912; died Dec. 30, 1919
Byron, William J. 1913–1919; died Dec. 27, 1955

Campbell, William M. 1939–40
Cantillon, Joseph D. 1902
Carpenter, William B. 1897, 1904, 1906–07
Clarke, Robert M. 1930–31
Cockill, George W. 1915; died Nov. 2, 1937
Colgan, Harry W. 1901
Colosi, Nicholas 1968–82

Conlan, John B. "Jocko" 1941–64; elected to Hall of Fame 1974; died April 16, 1989

Conway, John H. 1906

Crawford, Gerald J. 1976–present

Crawford, Henry C. "Shag" 1956–75;

Cunningham, Elmer E. 1901

Cusack, Stephen P. 1909

Cuzzi, Phil 1991–93

Dale, Jerry P. 1970–85

Dantley, Kerwin 1991–present

Darling, Gary R. 1988–present

Dascoli, Frank 1948–62; died Aug. 11, 1990

Davidson, David L. "Satch" 1969–84

Davidson, Robert A. 1983–present

Davis, Gerald 1985–present

Delmore, Victor 1956–59; died June 10, 1960

DeMuth, Dana 1986–present

Derr, Doll 1923

Dezelan, Frank J. 1966–68, 1969–71

Dixon, Hal H. 1953–59; died July 28, 1966

Donatelli, August J. 1950–73; died May 24, 1990

Donnelly, Charles H. 1931–32; died Dec. 13, 1968

Donohue, Michael R. 1930; died Aug. 7, 1968

Doyle, John J. 1911; died Dec. 31, 1958

Dreckman, Bruce 1996–

Dunn, Thomas P. 1939–46; died Jan. 20, 1976

Eason, Malcolm W. 1902, 1910–16

Engel, Robert A. 1965–90

Engeln, William R. 1952–56; died April 17, 1968

Fields, Stephen H. 1979–92

Finneran, William F. 1911–12, 1923–24; died July 30, 1961

Forman, Allen S. 1961–65

Frary, Ralph 1911; died Nov. 10, 1925

Froemming, Bruce 1971–present

Fyfe, Lee C. 1920

Gibbons, Brian 1994–present

Goetz, Lawrence J. 1936–57; died Oct. 31, 1962

Gore, Arthur J. 1947–56; died Sept. 29, 1986

Gorman, Brian 1991–present

Gorman, Thomas D. 1951–76; died Aug. 11, 1986

Gregg, Eric E. 1977–91, 1993–present

Guglielmo, A. Augie 1952; died February 1996

Guthrie, William J. 1913–1915; died March 6, 1950

Hallion, Thomas F. 1986–present

Harris, Lannie D. 1979–85; deceased

Harrison, Peter A. 1916–20; died March 9, 1921

Hart, Eugene F. 1920–29; died May 10, 1937

Hart, William F. 1914–15

Harvey, H. Douglas 1962–92

Henline, Walter J. 1945–48; died Oct. 9, 1957

Hernandez, Angel 1991–present

Hirschbeck, Mark 1986–present
Hohn, William J. 1987–present
Holliday, James W. 1903
Holmes, Howard 1921; died Sept. 18, 1945

Irwin, Arthur A. 1902

Jackowski, William A. 1952–68; died July 1996
Johnson, Henry S. "Steamboat" 1914; died Feb. 20, 1951
Johnstone, James E. 1903–12
Jorda, Louis D. 1927–31, 1940–52; died May 27, 1964

Kane, Stephen J. 1909–10
Kellogg, Jeffery 1991–present
Kennedy, Charles 1904
Kibler, John 1963–89
Klem, William J. 1905–41; died Sept. 1, 1951; elected to Hall of Fame 1953

Landes, Stanley A. 1955–72
Layne, Jerry B. 1989–present
Libbey, Stephen A. 1880
Lincoln, Frederick H. 1914, 1917
Long, Robert 1992

McCafferty, Charles 1921, 1923
McCormick, William J. "Barry" 1919–29; died Jan. 28, 1956
McGrew, Harry T. "Ted" 1930–31, 1933–34; died June 29, 1969
McLaughlin, Edward J. 1929; died Nov. 28, 1965
McLaughlin, Peter J. 1924–28

McSherry, John P. 1971 – 1996; died April 1, 1996
Magee, Sherwood R. 1928; died March 13, 1929
Magerkurth, George L. 1929–47; died Oct. 7, 1966
Marsh, Randall G. 1983–present
Meals, Gerry 1996
Montague, Edward M. 1976–present
Moran, August 1903–04, 1910, 1918
Moran, Charles B. 1917–39; died June 13, 1949
Mullin, John 1909

Nash, William M. 1901
Nauert, Paul 1996

O'Connor, Arthur 1914
O'Hara (no first name available), 1915
Olsen, Andrew H. 1968–81
O'Rourke, James H. 1894
Orth, Albert L. 1912–17
O'Sullivan, John J. 1922
Owens, Clarence B. "Brick" 1908, 1912–13

Pallone, David M. 1979–88
Parker, George L. 1936–38
Pelekoudas, Christos G. "Chris" 1960–75; died Nov. 30, 1984
Pfirman, Charles H. "Cy" 1922–36; died May 10, 1937
Pinelli, Ralph A. "Babe" 1935–56; died Oct. 22, 1984
Poncino, Larry L. 1986–88, 1991 – present
Potter, Scott 1991 – present
Powell, Cornelius J. "Jack" 1923–24, 1933; died July 25, 1971

Power, Charles B. 1902
Pryor, J. Paul 1961–81, died Oct.
 1996
Pulli, Frank V. 1972–present

Quick, James E. 1976–present
Quigley, Ernest C. 1913–37

Rapuano, Edward 1990–present
Reardon, John E. "Beans" 1926–49;
 died July 31, 1984
Reliford, Charles 1989–present
Rennert, Laurence H. "Dutch"
 1973–92
Rieker, Richard 1992–present
Rigler, Charles "Cy" 1906–22,
 1924–35
Rippley, T. Steven, 1985–present
Robb, Douglas W. "Scotty"
 1948–52; died April 10, 1969
Roberts, Leonard W. 1953–55
Rudderham, John E. 1908
Runge, Paul E. 1973–present
Ryan, Walter 1946; died June 16,
 1981

Scott, James 1930–31; died April 7,
 1957
Sears, John W. "Ziggy" 1934–45;
 died Dec. 16, 1956
Secory, Frank E. 1952–70; died
 April 7, 1995
Sentelle, Leopold T. "Paul" 1922–23
Smith, Vincent A. 1957–65; died
 Dec. 14, 1979
Stark, Albert D. "Dolly" 1928–35,
 1937–39, 1942; died Aug. 24,
 1968 Steiner, Melvin J. 1961–72
Steinfeldt, Harry M. 1905
Stello, Richard J. 1969–87; died
 Nov. 18, 1987

Sternburg, Paul, 1909
Stewart, William J. 1933–54; died
 Feb. 18, 1967
Stockdale, M.J. 1915
Sudol, Edward L. 1957–77
Sweeney, James M. 1924–26; died
 Jan. 29, 1950

Tata, Terry A. 1973–present
Terry, William H. "Adonnis" 1900
Tremblay, Richard H. 1971; died
 June 12, 1987
Truby, Harry G. 1909

Vanover, Larry, 1991, 1993–present
Vargo, Edward P. 1960–83
Venzon, Anthony 1957–71; died
 Sept. 20, 1971

Walsh, Francis D. 1961–63; died
 1985
Warneke, Lonnie 1949–55; died
 June 23, 1978
Wendelstedt, Harry H. 1966–present
West, Joseph H. 1976, 1978–present
Westervelt, Frederick E. 1922; died
 May 4, 1955
Weyer, Lee H. 1961, 1963–88; died
 July 4, 1988
Wickham, Daniel 1990–92
Williams, Arthur 1972–77; died
 Feb. 8, 1979
Williams, Charles H. 1978, 1983–
 present
Williams, William G. 1963–87
Wilson, Frank 1922–28; died June
 1928
Winters, Michael J. 1990–present

Zimmer, Charles L. "Chief" 1904

1900 to present: American League

Adams, John H. 1903
Anthony, G. Merlyn 1969–75
Ashford, Emmett L. 1966–70; died March 1, 1980
Avants, Nick R. 1969–71

Barnett, Lawrence R. 1968–present
Barrett, Ted 1994–present
Barry, Daniel 1928; deceased
Basil, Stephen 1936–42; died June 24, 1962
Bean, Ed 1994
Berry, Charles F. 1942–62; died Sept. 6, 1972
Betts, William G. 1901
Boyer, James M. 1944–50; died July 29, 1959
Bremigan, Nicholas G. 1974–88; died July 24, 1989
Brinkman, Joseph N. 1973–present

Campbell, William M. 1928–31
Cantillon, Joseph D. 1901
Carpenter William B. 1904
Carrigan, H. Sam 1961–65
Caruthers, Robert L. 1902–03
Cederstrom, Gary 1989–present
Chill, Oliver P. 1914–16, 1919–22
Chylak, Nestor L. 1954–78; died Feb. 17, 1982
Clark, Alan M. 1976–present
Coble, G. Drew 1983–present
Colliflower, James H. 1910; died Aug. 14, 1961

Connolly, Thomas H. 1901–31; elected to Hall of Fame 1953; died April 28, 1961
Connor, Thomas 1905–06
Cooney, Terrance J. 1975–92
Cooper, Eric 1996
Cousins, Derryl 1979–present
Craft, Terry 1989–present
Culbreth, Fieldin ("Phil") 1993–present

Deegan, William E. J. 1970–80
Denkinger, Donald A. 1968–present
DiMuro, Louis J. 1963–80; died June 7, 1982
DiMuro, Ray 1996
Dinneen, William H. 1909–37
Donnelly, Charles H. 1934–35; died Dec. 13, 1968
Doyle, Walter J. 1963; died March 2, 1988
Drummond, Calvin T. 1960–69; died May 2, 1970
Duffy, James F. 1951–55
Dwyer, J. Francis 1904

Egan, John J. "Rip" 1908–14
Eldridge, Clarence E. 1914–1915
Evans, James B. 1971–present
Evans, William G. 1906–27; died Jan. 23, 1956; elected to Hall of Fame 1973

Ferguson, Charles A. 1913; died May 17, 1931
Flaherty, John F. "Red" 1953–73
Ford, R. Dale 1975–present
Frantz, Arthur F. 1969–77

Friel, William E. 1920; died
Dec. 24, 1959
Froese, Grover A. 1952–53; died
July 20, 1982

Garcia, Richard R. 1975–present
Giesel, Harry C., 1925–42; died
Feb. 20, 1966
Goetz, Russell L. 1968–83
Grieve, William T. 1938–55; died
Aug. 17, 1979
Guthrie, William J. 1922, 1928–32;
died March 6, 1950

Haller, William E. 1961, 1963–82
Hart, Robert F. 1912–13
Hart, William F. 1901
Haskell, John E. 1901
Hassett, James E. 1903
Hayes, Gerald 1925–26
Hendry, Eugene "Ted" 1978–present
Herrichs, Jeff 1993
Hickox, Edward, 1990–present
Hildebrand, George A. 1912–34;
died May 30, 1960
Hirschbeck, John F. 1984–present
Holmes, Howard E. "Ducky"
1923–24; died Sept. 18, 1945
Honochick, G. James 1949–73; died
1994
Hubbard, R. Cal 1936–51, 1954–62;
elected to Hall of Fame 1976;
died Oct. 16, 1977
Hurley, Edwin H. 1947–65; died
Nov. 12, 1969
Hurst, Timothy C. 1905–09

Johnson, Mark S. 1984–present
Johnston, Charles E. 1936–37;
deceased

Johnstone, James E. 1902
Jones, Nicholas I. "Red" 1944–49;
died March 19, 1987
Joyce, James A. 1989–present

Kaiser, Kenneth J. 1977–present
Kelly, Thomas B. 1905
Kerin, John 1909–10
King, Charles F. 1904
Kinnamon, William E. 1960–69
Kolls, Louis C. 1933–40; died Feb.
23, 1941
Kosc, Gregory J. 1976–present
Kunkel, William G. 1968–84; died
May 4, 1985

Linsalata, Joseph N. 1961–62
Luciano, Ronald 1968–80; died
1994

McCarthy, John 1905
McClelland, Timothy R. 1984–
present
McCormick, William J. "Barry"
1917; died Jan. 28, 1956
McCoy, Larry S. 1970–present
McGowan, William A. 1925–54;
died Dec. 9, 1954; elected to Hall
of Fame 1992.
McGreevy, Edward 1912–13
McKean, James G. 1974–94
McKinley, William F. 1946–65;
died Aug. 1, 1980
Maloney, George P. 1968–83
Manassau, Alfred S. 1901
Marberry, Frederick "Firpo" 1935;
died June 30, 1976
Meriwether, Julius "Chuck" 1988–
present
Merrill, E. Durwood 1977–present

Morgenweck, Henry C. 1972–75
Moriarty, George J. 1917–26,
    1929–40; died April 8, 1964
Morrison, Daniel G. 1984–present
Mulaney, Dominic J. 1915; died
    Aug. 21, 1964
Mullin, John 1911–12

Nallin, Richard F. 1915–33; died
    Sept. 7, 1956
Napp, Larry A. 1951–74
Neudecker, Jerome A. "Jerry"
    1965–85; died Jan. 11, 1997

O'Brien, Joseph 1912, 1914; died
    Nov. 5, 1925
Odom, James C. 1965–74; died Jan.
    18, 1989
O'Donnell, James M. "Jake"
    1968–71
O'Laughlin, Francis H. "Silk"
    1902–18
O'Nora, Brian 1992–present
Ormsby Emmett T. "Red" 1923–41;
    died Oct. 11, 1962
Owens, Clarence B. "Brick"
    1916–37

Palermo, Stephen M. 1977–91
Paparella, Joseph J. 1946–65
Parker, Harley P. 1911
Parks, Dallas F. 1979–83
Passarella, Arthur M. 1941–42,
    1945–53; died Oct. 12, 1981
Perrine, Fred "Bull" 1909–12
Phillips, David R. 1971–present
Pipgras, George W. 1938–46; died
    Oct. 19, 1986

Quinn, John A. 1935–42, died July
    4, 1968

Reed, Rick A. 1984–present
Reilly, Michael E. 1978–present
Rice, John L. 1955–73
Robb, Douglas W. "Scotty"
    1952–53; died April 10, 1969
Rodriguez, Armando W. 1974–75
Roe, John "Rocky" 1982–94
Rommel, Edwin A. 1938–59; died
    Aug. 26, 1970
Rowland, Clarence H. "Pants"
    1923–27; died May 17, 1969
Rue, Joseph W. 1938–47; died Dec.
    1, 1984
Runge, Edward P. 1954–70

Salerno, Alexander J. 1961–68
Schwarts, Harry C. 1960–62; died
    Feb. 22, 1963
Scott, Dale A. 1986–present
Sheridan, John F. 1901–14
Shulock, John R. 1979–present
Smith, W. Alaric "Al" 1960–65
Soar, A. Henry "Hank" 1950–73
Spenn, Frederick C. 1979–80
Springstead, Martin J. 1965–86
Stafford, John H. 1907;
Stevens, John W. 1948–71; died
    Sept. 9, 1981
Stewart, Ernest D. 1941–45
Stewart, Robert D. 1959–70; died
    1982
Summers, William R. 1933–59;
    died Sept. 12, 1966

Tabacchi, Frank T. 1956–59; died
    Oct. 26, 1983
Tschida, Timothy J. 1986–present

Umont, Frank W. 1954–73; died
  June 20, 1981

Valentine, William T. 1963–68
Van Graflan Roy 1927–33; died
  Sept. 4, 1983
Voltaggio, Vito H. "Vic" 1977–present

Wallace, Roderick J. 1915–16
Walsh, Edward A. 1922; died May
  26, 1959

Weafer, Harold L. 1943–47; died
  Aug. 23, 1978
Welke, Timothy J. 1985–present
Westervelt, Frederick E. 1911–12;
  died May 4, 1955
Wilson, Frank 1921–22; died June
  1928
Winans, Mark 1994

Young, Larry E. 1985–94

Bibliography

Books

Charlton, Jim. *The Who, What, When, Where, Why and How of Baseball*. New York: Barnes & Noble, 1995.

Dittmar, Joseph J. *Baseball's Benchmark Boxscores*. Jefferson, N.C.: McFarland, 1990.

Gerlach, Larry R. *The Men in Blue*. Lincoln: University of Nebraska Press, 1980.

Gettelson, Leonard. *World Series Records*. St. Louis: The Sporting News, 1976.

Golenbock, Peter. *Wild, High and Tight: The Life and Death of Billy Martin*. New York: St. Martin's Press, 1994.

Johnson, Harry. *Standing the Gaff*. Nashville: Parthenon Press, 1935.

Kaufman, Louis; Barbara Fitzgerald, and Tom Sewell. *Moe Berg: Athlete, Scholar...and Spy*. Boston: Little, Brown & Company, 1972.

Libby, Bill. *Catfish: The Three Million Dollar Pitcher*. New York: Coward, McCann & Geoghegan, 1976.

Marazzi, Rich. *The Rules and Lore of Baseball*. New York: Stein and Day, 1980.

Newhan, Ross. *The California Angels: A Complete History*. New York: Simon & Schuster, 1982.

Obojski, Robert. *Bush League*. New York: Macmillan, 1975.

Okrent, Daniel and Harris Lewine. *The Ultimate Baseball Book*. Boston: Houghton Mifflin, 1988.

O'Neal, Bill. *The Texas League: A Century of Baseball*. Austin: Eakin Press, 1987.

Peary, Danny. *We Played The Game*. New York: Hyperion, 1994.

Reichler, Joseph L. *The Baseball Encyclopedia*. New York: Macmillan, 1986.

Reidenbaugh, Lowell. *Baseball's Hall of Fame: Cooperstown, Where the Legends Live*. New York: Arlington House, 1986.

Skipper, James K. *Baseball Nicknames: A Dictionary of Origins and Meanings*. Jefferson, N.C.: McFarland, 1992.

Skipper John C. *Inside Pitch: A Closer Look at Classic Baseball Moments*. Jefferson, N.C.: McFarland, 1996.

Smalling, R.J. *The Sport Americana Baseball Address List*. Cleveland: Edgewater Book Co., 1992.

Smith, Curt. *The Storytellers*. New York. Macmillan, 1995.

Smith, Ron. *The Sporting News Chronicle of Baseball*. New York: BDD Illustrated Books, 1993.

Society for American Baseball Research. *Baseball Research Journal*. Cooperstown, NY, 1979; 1980; 1981; 1982.

Thorn, John and Pete Palmer. *Total Baseball*. New York: Warner Books, 1989.

Wurman, Richard Saul. *Baseball Access*. Los Angeles: Access Press Limited, 1984.

Newspapers

Hull, Dave. "Pioneers Nip Springfield in 27 Innings; Longest Marathon in Baseball's History." *The Elmira* (N.Y.) *Sunday Telegram*, May 9, 1965.

Miller, Dick. "Ryan's Pace: Four No-Hitters in Two-Year Span." *The Sporting News*, June 14, 1975.

Pepe, Phil. "Little Bucky Is Yanks' Mr. Big in Clutch." *The Sporting News*, Oct. 14, 1978.

"Fernando Saluted for Gritty Performance." *The Sporting News*, Nov. 7, 1981.

Ray, Ralph. "Cincy's Riverfront Gang Runs Off with Loot." *The Sporting News*, Oct. 17, 1970.

Index